ADVOCACY SKILLS

Contents

To I. J. H.

and R. H.

In Memoriam

Preface

I have added for this edition some more precepts and examples, particularly regarding preparation, submissions and questioning. I have also discussed what I believe to be the new style of advocacy which concentrates on brevity. I have given an example in Appendix 2 of a skeleton argument. Examples of these dry bones are hard to come by. I hope that the example I have provided will form an adaptable model.

In this edition I have tried to deal with some specific problems which have been experienced by students in their advocacy exercises. How to make submissions is a prime example.

As the emphasis is placed in this edition on the desirability of brevity, I shall conclude.

Michael Hyam
Suffolk
June 1995

Preface to the Second Edition

I have added a short chapter on what I have termed non adversarial advocacy. I have tried to show that the general principles of advocacy advanced in this book can easily be adapted to the type of advocacy where confrontation is out of place.

I should like to thank all those, too numerous to mention by name, who have made constructive criticisms of this book since it was published two years ago. I like to think that it has achieved one of its aims already, namely to stimulate thought about advocacy and its technique. I hope that it will continue to do so, and will take its place among those books which are of material help to the aspiring advocate.

Michael Hyam
Suffolk
March 1992

Preface to the First Edition

It is sometimes said that advocates are born and not made. This book has been written in the belief that anybody with the patience to work at it can become a competent advocate by learning the principles of the art. There is, after all, a technique in every art which has to be learnt by its practitioners. Even Mozart had to learn the technique of composition.

Once the technical skills of advocacy have been acquired those with more than ordinary talent and flair may go on to become outstanding advocates but even the less talented can be assured of being able to do a competent job. I have attempted in this book to show by analysis, example, and precept the direction in which the practising advocate should go in order to become effective and assured. My aim has been to stimulate thought about advocacy and to show that many of its daunting difficulties may be resolved by good preparation, which includes carefully thinking out what the case requires. The purpose of providing numerous examples is to enable the reader to use them as models which can be applied in a multitude of circumstances. I have also tried to show how the advocate can approach any particular problem by formulating an hypothesis which accounts for all the facts in the case. You will see, particularly in the chapter on cross-examination, what an effective tool this can be. In the last chapter I have put in summary form many of the lessons I have learnt about advocacy from hard experience.

Michael Hyam
Suffolk
May 1990

One

Learning to Speak

> *In the innocence of second childhood Mr Justice*
> *Shallow said to Ancient Pistol: 'If, Sir, you come with*
> *news from the Court, I take it there's but two ways —*
> *either to utter them or to conceal them'. That as other*
> *children say was all that Shallow knew. For uttering of*
> *them alone, there are three ways, apart from all the*
> *ways of concealing them. At any rate there are three*
> *ways of trying to make them attractive when uttered.*
> *You may state them about twice as big as they are, or*
> *about half as big as they are, or, if you have skill and*
> *complete confidence in your skill, you may state them*
> *just as big as they are. (A Writer's Notes on his Trade*
> *C. E. Montague, p. 44.)*

Although this book is primarily intended for those who are practising
advocates, or those who intend to practise, this first chapter is a general
introduction to speaking, and suggests a way in which anyone can learn
to speak fluently and effectively in public.

Everyone at the start of a speaking career would like to be able to speak
fluently, preferably without notes; but very few beginners would trust
themselves to try. Most feel the need to write out what they are going to
say in its entirety. The reason for doing this is understandable; you feel
that by doing so you will familiarise your mind with the subject-matter
of the speech, and then you will be able to get through all right. You will

also have the text of your speech in front of you if you lose your way. But this method of preparation should be avoided. If you have begun to speak in this way you would be well advised to abandon it. The reason for such emphatic advice is that this method has too many disadvantages to be satisfactory.

If you are a beginner, and you have the manuscript of your speech in front of you, you will be looking down, after the first few moments trying to find the place. When you do find it, it will be almost impossible to look up for fear of losing your place again. The result will probably be that you will read the whole of the speech. In court, it may be that the judge will interrupt you; that will create further difficulties, and you are likely to end in complete disarray. If you do not have the text in front of you, but none the less have previously written down the whole speech, you will find that you will be constantly saying to yourself 'I put it much better when I wrote it down' and you will be fumbling for your original words. The greatest disadvantage of all is that you will be so tied to what you have written down that you will be inhibited in thinking on your feet. It does not matter how experienced you are, inevitably you will find that your thoughts will focus and refocus on what you have previously written down; some alternative must therefore be found.

The alternative method must enable you to familiarise your mind with the subject-matter of the speech so that you can speak mainly from your head, although you will probably need to have trigger notes at hand as an aid to memory. There is no objection to using such notes if you need to do so, but there are some experienced speakers who find it more effective to speak without the use of notes.

This description of what is to be aimed at may at first sight appear too daunting to the beginner; but, even if you are a beginner you should reflect that you already can speak, and no doubt already have spoken, fluently without notes. Perhaps the last time you went to a party, a topic came up in the conversation in which you have a long-standing interest. You will have had no difficulty at all in speaking easily on that subject, and you may have felt a glow of satisfaction that you expressed yourself well. It is worth noting that when you spoke on that special subject you adapted your thoughts and the way in which you expressed them to suit the particular occasion and company, relying on your everyday vocabu-lary, without an attempt to speak in any style but your own. The reason why you were able to express yourself so fluently was because the subject was so familiar to your mind that there was, so to speak, a groove along which your thought ran.

From this illustration you may infer that if you can familiarise your mind with the subject in hand to the same degree that it is familiar with a pet subject you will be able to speak fluently without anything more than trigger notes. The method by which you can effectively familiarise your mind with any subject on which you may be required to speak is comparatively simple; and one which is easy to practise.

There are two essential steps in the process of making the groove in your mind; the most important of which is to think out the ideas you want to express. This advice might appear too obvious to be worth stating, and yet on the other hand it *must* be stated and dwelt on. Most of us are very lazy in the way in which we think about new information. By cursory reading we take in the gist of an article but if asked to express the ideas contained in the piece we should find it very hard to do so.

Take another illustration. You go to a lecture. It is on a difficult subject. You are paying close attention and making notes. After the lecture a friend comes up and asks you to explain a particular point. You think that you can do so, but when you try you get stuck. You find that you cannot get from point A in the argument to point B. You then have to go to the lecture notes and go through the thought processes of the lecturer before you can make the connection between A and B. This is a process of understanding, and it is only when the mind has gone through that process, looking at the width, breadth, and depth of an idea, that you can truly say that you have thought it through.

Turning again to the illustration of the lecture you will find that if, after referring to the notes, you try to explain the point immediately you will be able to do so, but probably haltingly. If you were to do so after an hour or two during which time it has been turned over in your mind you will be able to speak far more fluently. Another thing will also be noticed. If you express the idea once it will be much easier to do so again. After two or three occasions the subject will be perfectly clear in your mind. In short, the groove will have been made.

When you are learning the method of preparation which is being suggested you will find that expressing to a friend the more difficult ideas of your speech will be very effective in making the groove in your mind. There is however a further advantage in talking over your ideas; when you do so, new aspects of the subject will present themselves to your mind while you are speaking. You have very probably experienced it in ordinary conversation.

When Francis Bacon remarks in his *Essay on Friendship*, 'it is better for a man to speak to a statue or picture, than to suffer his thought to pass

in smother' he evidently meant that expression clarifies thought. For he
says in that *Essay* '... certain it is that whosoever hath his mind fraught
with many thoughts, his wits and understanding do clarify and break up
in the communicating and discoursing with another: he tosseth his
thoughts more easily; he marshalleth them more orderly; he seeth how
they look when they are turned into words: finally he waxeth wiser than
himself; and that more by an hour's discourse than by a day's
meditation.'

Although talking over your ideas with a friend is so useful in
familiarising your mind with the subject you will find with experience
that you will be able to think out how to express your ideas effectively
even without talking them over.

You should aim at creating a picture of the speech in your head; its
form, its logical structure and the connections between one idea and
another.

This simple illustration may be used as a model for a long speech, or
for preparation of parts of a speech. It is particularly useful when you
have to think out an important sub-argument in the speech and need to
have the sequence of the argument in precise order.

Suppose that you want to persuade your audience, drawn from the
villages in your area, to plant trees. You want them to realise that to do
so would be attainable, affordable and a practicable contribution to the
improvement of the environment. Your argument is designed to remove
any objections they may have to such a scheme based on imaginary
difficulties, and to spur them on to action.

The key words on which your argument is founded are: 'attainable',
'affordable', and 'practicable contribution'. The scheme is attainable
because you are proposing that each village should plant four trees each
year for three years; the labour in planting and maintenance is slight,
especially when shared, and problems of siting can easily be negotiated
with the farmer or the rector. The scheme is inexpensive; you can plant
acorns if you wish. The environmental advantages of planting trees are
universally accepted.

The key words will call to mind each of the ideas to be expressed in
the argument once it has been thought through; and by those words you
may hold in your mind's eye the whole speech including the points of
transition between one idea and another.

At this point it is as well to deal with two objections which may have
occurred to you. The first is that as we have to think out in words the ideas
we wish to express in a speech, the very act of thinking out the ideas will

be just as bad as writing down those words. The difference, however, seems to lie in the act of writing. When you write, you search for the precise word. You spend time on the construction of your sentences and even paragraphs, and in that way you become tied to what you have written. If that process happens at all when you think out your ideas in your head, there is no practical effect. You will certainly find that you will not be tied to the words you used in thinking out the idea. But a word of caution, don't rehearse your speech in front of a mirror, or try to rehearse the precise words you are going to use in your speech, because that does have the same effect as writing it out.

The second possible objection to the method so far described is that if you have expressed the idea in conversation, or spoken on the subject before, whenever you speak on the subject it will be no more than a dull rehash of what you have said previously. This danger can be avoided by developing your ideas, rearranging your thoughts and always trying to improve your presentation.

Lawyers like an authority almost as much as a reason, so a quotation from Quintilian is appropriate to confirm what has so far been advanced. In Book X VII 32 of *Institutio Oratoria* he says: 'For my own part I think that we should never write out anything which we do not intend to commit to memory. For if we do, our thoughts will run back to what we have elaborated in writing and will not permit us to try the fortune of the moment. Consequently, the mind will waver in doubt between the two alternatives, having forgotten what was committed to writing and being unable to think of anything fresh to say.'

I now turn to the arrangement of the ideas which you wish to express. At an early stage of preparation you must identify the argument which will be advanced in your speech, because it is a fundamental principle that effective speaking must be couched in the form of an argument. The word argument is here used to mean not only a connected series of statements or reasons intended to establish a position, but also to mean a theme or subject. The advantages of using the form of an argument are that, first, it will provide you with a tool to cut into the amorphous mass of material with which you are confronted. For example, you will see in the chapter on mitigation, that you will be searching for an argument based on principle, and you will use the facts of the case to point the argument. Secondly, as soon as the argument has been formulated the process of thinking out its logical sequence and bearings will greatly assist in the making of the groove in your mind. Thirdly, the logical sequence will be an aid to memory; and finally, the presentation of a flowing and coherent argument enables your hearers to understand what you are saying.

Once you have identified your argument, it should be constructed and developed by asking yourself intelligent questions, testing the validity of the argument, identifying weaknesses, silencing tacit objections and thinking how to present it with the maximum clarity.

It follows from what has already been suggested that the nearer you come to the moment of delivery of the speech the clearer the subject will be in your mind, but the final problem is the way in which you are to express your speech. The short answer is that you should use your everyday vocabulary.

There are several reasons for stressing the importance of using your everyday vocabulary. It will enable you to speak naturally and convincingly and so avoid the fault of many speakers who feel compelled to adopt an artificial manner of expression; the result is often bombastic and full of 'waffle'. You will also find that it will enable you to speak with spontaneity and freshness which is very hard to achieve otherwise. Perhaps most important of all, it will free you from the necessity of thinking out the precise words you are going to use, which would be subject to the dangers already discussed.

We have now reached the difficult subject of style. How can the beginner or even the fairly experienced speaker set about acquiring an attractive speaking style? The beginner may be apprehensive at the thought of stringing together sentence after sentence which may be ungrammatical, or fearful of getting stuck in mid-sentence with no apparent means of finishing. No doubt this will happen sometimes to begin with; but you must not be put off. Constant practice will put you right and all the time your confidence will increase. It is, however, after you have learnt to speak with reasonable fluency that the true art of advocacy comes into play. How do you set about creating a style of speaking which suits your personality and will be appropriate to the subjects on which you will be called upon to speak?

Justice Holmes in a letter to Lewis Einstein described style most felicitously: 'Style at bottom, of course, is a question of totals not of simple words. It is the personal equation of the writer. You have not quite reached yours yet. Your writing is not quite pure spontaneous glee. When the style is fully formed, if it has a sweet undersong we call it beautiful, and the writer may do what he likes in words or syntax; the material is plastic in his hands to image himself, which is all that anyone can give.' He thus describes the aim of the writer which applies equally to the speaker.

Cervantes in his preface to *Don Quixote* says: 'Do but take care to express yourself in a plain easy manner, in well chosen, significant and decent terms, and to give a harmonious and pleasing tone to your periods: study to explain your thoughts and set them in the truest light, labouring as much as possible not to leave them dark or intricate, but clear and intelligible.' G. B. Shaw in his *Advice to a Young Critic* had this to say: 'Always find out rigidly and exactly what you mean and never strike an attitude, whether national or moral or critical or anything else . . . get your facts right first; that is the foundation of all style, as you cannot express yourself genuinely except on the basis of precise reality.' Finally there is the severe injunction of Confucius: 'If language is not correct, then what is said is not what is meant; if what is said is not what is meant, then what ought to be done is left undone.'

The dominant idea which emerges from these quotations, varied as they are in language and period, is that style is the accurate expression of clear thought which should be achieved by the use of simple and harmonious words.

The acquisition of such a style, the cultivation of the art of expression, must necessarily be the pursuit of a lifetime; but we can all start today, if we have not begun already.

Your objective will be to develop a rich and idiomatic vocabulary. This does not mean knowing and using a lot of long words that nobody else understands. It means being able to express every nuance of meaning that you wish to express. You have to learn the 'weight and edge' of words; you also have to know something of the structure of the language. With this regard Somerset Maugham says in his essay *After Reading Burke*:

The manner of writing changes with the fleeting generations and it would be absurd to try to write now like one of the great stylists of the eighteenth century . . . but I see no reason to suppose that they have not something to teach us that may be to our purpose. The language of literature maintains its vitality by absorbing the current speech of the people: this gives it colour, vividness, and actuality; but if it is to avoid shapelessness and incoherence it must be founded on, and determined by, the standards of the period when English prose attained the highest degree of perfection of which it seems capable.

One of the most valuable things that can be learnt from Burke is that however unmanageable certain words may appear, it is possible by proper placing, the judicious admixture of long ones with short, by alternation of consonants and vowels and by alternation of accent, to secure euphony. Of course no one could write at all if he bore these considerations in mind; the ear does the work. In Burke's case I think it is evident that the natural sensibility of the organ was infinitely developed by the exigencies of public speech; even when he wrote only to read the sound of the spoken phrase was present to him.

It was Lord Macmillan who said in his essay 'Some Observations on the Art of Advocacy', *Law and Other Things*, Cambridge University Press, 1937, p. 200: 'I believe that no advocate can be a great pleader who has not a sense of literary form, and whose mind is not stored with the treasures of our great literary inheritance upon which he may draw at will. The fortune of an argument depends much more than is commonly realised on the literary garb in which it is presented. A point made in attractive language sticks in the judicial memory. You must avoid the commonplace without falling into the bizarre. Originality is effective but eccentricity merely repels.'

This advice sets a very high standard which will only be achieved by study and patience, and you may be wondering how you can set out on the path which leads to the breezy slopes of the 'Delectable Mountains' with some prospect of getting there. The answer lies in taking short steps and stopping every now and then to see how far you have come.

The first practical thing that can be done is to school yourself to speak accurately and correctly in ordinary conversation. In a well-known passage Boswell recalled how Sir Joshua Reynolds asked Dr Johnson by what means he had attained his extraordinary accuracy and flow of language. 'He told him he had early laid it down as a fixed rule to do his best on every occasion, and in every company: to impart whatever he knew in the most forcible language he could put it in: and that by constant practice, and never suffering any careless expressions to escape him, or attempting to deliver his thoughts without arranging them in the clearest manner, it became habitual to him.' Every speaker might well follow that example.

Careful attention should be given to the acquisition of idiomatic vocabulary. I mean by this not only to avoid solecisms, but an ability to use the language which is appropriate to your subject. It hardly needs saying that this is not an exhortation to use jargon; on the contrary that should have no place in your vocabulary. Legal concepts sometimes have to be expressed by use of terms of art. The lawyer must be able to use these as a workman uses his tools. The quickest way of learning the vocabulary of the law is regularly to read the law reports. Many of our Judges, past and present, use the language with power and precision, and there is much to learn from their judgments about the way in which legal principles should be stated and the way in which the facts and law in the particular case should be arranged so as to make the presentation easily understood.

Clarity alone is not advocated as the hallmark of style. There is such a thing as too much clarity; it has a cold clatter. Clearness at any price should be avoided. The type of clarity that I am warning against is that pedantry which consists in giving too precise an account than the subject demands. We have met it often enough: 'On the twenty-third day of March one thousand nine hundred and ninety five anno Domini, Mr John Duke Smith was walking, or perhaps trotting, but certainly not ambling, along the road or pathway...'. The speaker seems to hymn 'Nothing in my brain I bring'. In any vivid picture there should be plenty of contrast — a detailed exposition where the argument demands it, but artful summary of background information. 'Were it not so, we might find our best light reading in Acts of Parliament, because their whole aim in life is to be clear; the same bright, even light beats shadowlessly down upon every square inch of their level expanses of verbiage. Yet most of us find them plain stuff in the worse sense as well as the better.' (C. E. Montague.)

On this general question of style let Quintilian have the last word, for although he speaks with the authority of centuries his words are as apt today as they were when he wrote them (*loc. cit.,* Book VIII 22):

The usual result of over-attention to the niceties of style is the deterioration of our eloquence. The main reason for this is that those words are best which are least far fetched and give the impression of simplicity and reality. For those words which are obviously the result of careful search and even seem to parade their self conscious art, fail to attain the grace at which they aim and lose all appearance of sincerity because they darken the sense.... For in our passion for words we paraphrase what might be said in plain language, repeat what we have already said at sufficient length, pile up a number of words where one would suffice, and regard allusion as better than directness of speech... and yet Cicero, long since laid down this rule in the clearest language, that the worst fault in speaking is to adopt a style inconsistent with the idiom of ordinary speech and contrary to the common feeling of mankind.

Two

Preparation

Reflect, gentleman, how many disputes you must have listened to, which were interminable because neither party understood either his opponent or himself. (Cardinal Newman, 1858)

Good advocacy depends on good preparation. It is necessary to prepare your case by taking both a general and specific view of it; so that you have clear in your mind not only what you have to prove or disprove, but also the way in which you are going to do it.

It is essential for you to have a thorough knowledge of the law of evidence and procedure, otherwise you will be handicapped at every turn by uncertainty as to whether a piece of evidence is admissible, whether it has to be proved by oral evidence, whether, if it is contained in a document, it is necessary to call the maker of it and so forth. Much of this knowledge should and will become almost instinctive, but it is, of course, necessary to have a thorough working knowledge of even the more unusual points of evidence and procedure. The reason is that this is the only branch of the law in which there is often no opportunity to research a point, because it comes up unexpectedly and calls for an instant response. Take, as an obvious example, an issue as to whether a piece of evidence is or is not hearsay; you may have to object to it as it is about to be led. You must be able to recognise it immediately as hearsay and to formulate your objection. Take an instance which frequently occurs. It has become a widely adopted practice for advocates to deal with evidence by a device which is loosely thought to evade the hearsay rule. The witness is asked 'Now don't tell us what was said, but what did you do as a result of speaking to the man'. This formula is objectionable because what was said by the man may be inferred from what the witness did. If what was said was relevant, it was hearsay and if it was irrelevant it was inadmissible anyway. Frequently when this device is used it is of no consequence, but sometimes damaging hearsay evidence is brought in. You must be able to object to the evidence being given in this way, first by recognising that it is inadmissible, and secondly by being able to formulate the objection in a compelling way. You can do so by stating the reason and the authority, *Glinsky* v *McIver* [1972] AC 772. (You will see the way in which this objection can be made in Chapter 3 at page 30.)

At an early stage of preparation you may be required to advise on evidence. You will have to consider whether additional evidence should be sought, whether more investigations should be carried out, whether it will be necessary to serve notice on the other side under the Civil Evidence Act 1968 to use a document in evidence, and the like. It is evident that in order to advise properly you will need a very detailed knowledge of the case you have to make and that which you have to disprove. But regardless of whether or not you need to advise on evidence, the steps in preparation are the same. You must have a detailed and exact knowledge of the facts of your case and the law that applies to it.

In your first reading of the papers it is sufficient if you get your bearings. From the outset it is useful to have in mind these two questions:

(a)   What has to be proved or disproved?
(b)   How is your case to be proved and your opponent's disproved?

Once you have a clear idea of the issues, which you will pick up on your first reading, you will be able to distinguish what is relevant in the brief and what is not. With practice this is a facility which will enable you to master a case with ease and rapidity. But bear this caution in mind; do not skip over what you think is likely to be irrelevant. Read everything. Sometimes you will find buried in a mass of irrelevance a crucial fact which may make the difference between winning and losing, and it lies buried because no one else has seen its significance.

It is most useful, in fact essential, to prepare a chronology of events as soon as you begin your preparation of the facts in earnest. This will not only be useful during the preparation of the case but also as an aid to memory to guide you when presenting the case in court. It is a common experience to find when you compile the chronology that a pattern of events emerges which you would not otherwise discern. For example, in a case where a man was charged with smashing windows in crematoriums in various parts of the home counties, a chronology of breakings revealed that on five separate occasions two breakings had occurred the same night at places far apart. As the prosecution contended that the defendant was a vagrant relying on public transport, the facts suggested that more than one person was involved. It was only when the breakings were put into date order that the point could be appreciated.

When you are coming to grips with the facts of the case it is essential that you go beyond a simple recognition of the allegations of fact on either side. Your aim should be to see and understand what really happened and you should do it by analysing the facts with which you are presented. It is necessary to draw inferences from the primary facts and to formulate an hypothesis which will enable you to gain a true understanding of the case. An illustration of what is meant can be taken from the Morland case. (Sir Patrick Hastings' speech in his defence is to be found in Appendix 1 at page 176 with a short explanation of what the case was about.) The Attorney-General in his preparation must have foreseen that the defence of Morland was going to be a justification of the words used in certifying the balance sheets. He must have known that the form of words used would be approved by eminent members of the accountancy profession. His argument was that the balance sheets of the company were in fact false in that they misrepresented the company's affairs. His hypothesis was that knowing that the balance sheets were false Morland had cunningly hit upon a form of words to justify the balance sheets; but the form of words was in fact no more than a mask, very skilfully worn, to provide a justification if challenged. He was, as it turned out, unsuccessful in convincing the jury that this meant Morland had committed the offence alleged, but it enabled him to know what evidence to collate in order to present a prima facie case.

When formulating an hypothesis of this kind it is essential for great care to be used. The inferences which are drawn from primary facts must be necessary inferences and not mere guesswork. You must have due regard to the ethical rules which dictate what an advocate may do. For example, in defending a person charged with a criminal offence, you must not, needless to say, invent a defence where none existed, or where an inferior defence existed, devise a better one. In the chapter on cross-examination examples are given of the legitimate use of an hypothesis based entirely on inferences drawn from the primary facts of the case.

Like any hypothesis in any field of speculation, it must accommodate and explain all the known facts. When you are formulating it you must pay close attention to every detail which might be relevant. When you come upon an unmalleable fact, you must enlarge your hypothesis to explain it. If you cannot, you will have to abandon the hypothesis.

Another aspect of general preparation is researching the law which applies to the case. That must also be done with thoroughness. When you are researching a point of law, work it through to a conclusion before passing to the next point. In a complex matter, where there are many tangled questions to be resolved, it is a good idea to make notes of all points which may be relevant. They need only be trigger notes, so long as you have the precise reference. It often happens that at one stage of preparation you do not appreciate the significance of a particular point. You may then think it of only marginal relevance, but later on it may assume a greater importance and you do not want to waste valuable time in hunting the reference down because you did not bother to note it at first.

It may be thought that these suggestions are all very well if there were unlimited time available for preparation; but as everyone with any experience of litigation knows, you often have to get a case up at very short notice. What then? The main difficulty is doing your research on the law. It is useful if you have been able to prepare beforehand for such emergencies. I found it of real practical value to keep an index of cases relevant to the field in which I practised. Such an index should be compiled according to subject-matter, or by reference to a key word which is likely to linger in the memory, rather than according to case name. For example, if you have 'seat belts' in your index and there list all the cases which deal with damages in seat belt cases, you will be able to find the authorities you want immediately. As a safeguard you might also have an entry in your index 'contributory negligence' and the seat belt cases would also be referred to under this head. All that is necessary to work this system is to obtain two card-indexes. In one you keep the subject references, and write across the page the numbers 0–9 inclusive. In the other index you write the name of the case at the top, and its reference in the law reports and the card number, the last figure of which corresponds with the subject reference numbers. At the bottom of the case card you write the key word(s), in our example, seat belts/ contributory negligence. Thus, you look up 'seat belts'; you find references on that card to card numbers, 5, 20, and 32. You go to those numbers in the other index and have the relevant cases with their names and references in the reports immediately available. The main advantage of this system is that it enables you to find the case which you naggingly half remember. The system can also be used to note the statement of general or specific principles of law which are otherwise difficult to track down. For example, what is the meaning and ambit of the phrase 'without prejudice'.

A much better, more efficient and up-to-date system is available on computer; and all the time more reports are coming on line on *cd-rom*. The whole of the Weekly Law Reports are now available. All you have to do is to look up a word or phrase, say 'seat belts', and in a matter of a few seconds all the reports where the phrase is mentioned come up on screen. This facility is clearly ideal for lawyers, and cuts down on laborious research.

Preparation and presentation depend on orderliness. At the outset you should put, and then keep, your papers in good order. Weed out irrelevant documents and put them aside. Put the relevant documents in chronological order, or if chronology is not appropriate, into logical order. Marginal references are always useful, and many people favour highlighting in different colours, the colours corresponding with a party to the proceedings, or a line of argument or the like. Cross-referencing should be employed as a means of making sure that a fleeting allusion hidden in some obscure place is correlated with the main body of the evidence.

In preparing the case for court it may be that there are hundreds or thousands of pages of documents. It is difficult to overstress how important it is to have the documents sorted out so that it is easy to find the document you want. Your particular concern as you conduct the case is to make sure that the tribunal will be able to follow your presentation of it. Make sure that the bundles of documents are not too large; it helps to keep the judge at a low irritability level if he can handle the bundles easily, if they are arranged logically, if the bundles from which the advocates are working have the same page numbers (how often they do not!), if plans are of a convenient size to handle, if photostats are legible and if there is a comprehensive index. These points make all the difference to the smooth running of the case.

Take for example a fraud case. If you have a say in the preparation of the bundles (and you should have), you will have to decide whether to refer to the documents by the exhibit number as well as by the page number. Views differ, but for reference I prefer to use page numbers only. When you are presenting the case it is much simpler to have to refer only to one set of numbers. It is a good idea also, if there are a large number of bundles, to have the covers of each bundle in a different colour. That again makes for ease of handling. Always make sure that the documents in the bundles are presented in a comprehensible order; preferably in the order in which you intend to refer to them in the presentation of your case. It is very difficult to hold the attention of a tribunal, whether judge or jury, if you constantly have to flit from bundle to bundle in order to establish a single point.

In *B* v *B* [1994] 1 FLR 323, Mr Justice Wall gave guidelines for the preparation of bundles of documents. He pointed out that the preparation of court bundles was an essential element in the art of advocacy. The guidelines were as follows:

1.   Preparation of bundles by solicitors:—

Should be done in consultation with Counsel.

Must be done in consultation with solicitors for all other parties.

Must be done in good time before trial.

2.   It is the responsibility of the applicant solicitor or fee earner having the conduct of the case, to check bundles before they leave the office. This responsibility should not lie with junior office staff.

3.   All documents must be legible and not abbreviated.

4.   Documents must be in a logical (usually chronological) order, the oldest at the top.

5.   All bundles must be properly indexed with a description of each document and the page number at which it begins and ends.

6.   Pagination should be consecutive and continuous throughout each bundle and should not for example refer to 'page 1 of 3'. Copy bundles should be made after a master bundle has been paginated.

7.   It is preferable for solicitors having the conduct of the litigation to prepare and distribute all the bundles and to charge for photocopying. . . .

8.   Whilst each case varies in relation to the issues that arise from it, thought should always be given to the categorisation of documents and their distribution into individual documents and their distribution into individual bundles. . . .

9.   [Medical records and solicitors' letters should be in chronological order.] [I have summarised this paragraph.]

10.   [not reproduced]

11.   Wherever possible the chronology prepared by the applicant should be cross referenced to the relevant page in the relevant bundle.... A *dramatis personae* which identifies the parties and the principal witnesses and where their evidence is to be found is extremely useful to the judge.

The remainder of the direction deals with detailed points of presentation which need not take up room here. You would be well advised to look at the complete direction if preparing a case for presentation in court.

It is part of preparation nowadays to formulate a skeleton argument. There is an art of doing this effectively so as to assist the court and at the same time to leave sufficient room for manoeuvre in the course of the presentation of your case in Court.

The rules regarding the preparation of skeleton arguments are set out in the White Book; and in practice directions. Broadly speaking, the principle is that you must make plain, succinctly, what the range of your arguments is and the pith of them.

In the Chancery Guide issued by Scott V-C in April 1995, Appendix 3, at p. 73, sets out guidelines on the content of skeleton arguments:

1.   A skeleton argument should:

(1)   concisely summarise the party's submissions in relation to each of the issues. It should cite the main authorities relied upon, which may be attached. It is not however the function of a skeleton argument to argue the case on paper.

(2)   be as brief as the nature of the issues allows. It should not normally exceed 20 pages of double spaced A4 paper and in many cases it should be much shorter than this.

(3)   be divided into numbered paragraphs and paged consecutively. Any additional skeleton arguments coming from the same party should continue the numbering from the end of the previous document.

(4)   avoid formality and make use of abbreviations, e.g., P for Plaintiff; A/345 for bundle A page 345, 1.1.95 for 1st. January 1995 etc.

2.   These guidelines apply also to written summaries of opening speeches and final speeches.

These guidelines were specifically designed for use in the Chancery Division, but are of general application.

I am indebted to Mr Gregory Stone QC for an example of a skeleton argument in a planning case which may be found in Appendix 2. Here, for brevity, is a summary of the main ingredients and ordering of the argument:

1. *Introduction*   This states succinctly the main issues before the court.

2. *Legal framework*   This outlines the law applicable. You will appreciate that the tribunal will often be familiar with the scope of the relevant law, but will not necessarily have in mind the precise wording of the statute, or precisely what the relevant cases say. So in mounting your skeleton argument you should state succinctly the relevant wording of that part of the statute on which you rely; or an accurate summary of the principles stated in the cases on which you rely. Giving the legal framework before the factual background to the case has the advantage of enabling the tribunal to see what is legally relevant as the facts unfold. By putting the legal framework first the judge can see how the development of the argument is supported by the facts.

3. *Background*   This enables you to state broadly the factual basis of the case. Care should be taken to make this sufficiently detailed to be readily comprehensible but not over weighted with the *minutiae* of the case. Effectively this should if possible be an agreed factual basis. If it cannot or has not been agreed the common ground between the parties should be outlined and the actual issues which are in dispute stated compendiously.

4. *Submissions*   This should set out your broad argument but leave room for manoeuvre.

5. *Conclusion*   This should summarise the effect of your argument and the relief claimed.

Another aspect of preparation which has come to the fore in criminal as well as in civil cases is the question of discovery, when there may be an issue as to public interest immunity or professional privilege.

The preparation of a criminal case often needs the most careful investigation by the prosecution of what ought to be disclosed to the defence as unused material. The rules about disclosure have been authoritatively stated in the case of *Ward* 96 Cr App R 1 and in the case of *Davies and Johnson* 97 Cr App R 110. It is not sufficient for the

advocate who has the conduct of the case in court to rely entirely on his
instructions, or on what the police have supplied. Assuming the bona
fides of the police and those instructing you, it may sometimes happen
that a source of important unused material is not identified, or has been
overlooked. Say, for example, in a case of affray; you as the advocate will
want to know whether any negative statements by witnesses at the scene
were taken by the police. The fact that a number of witnesses did not see
or hear anything relating to the incident, when if anything had happened
they may have been expected to have done so, is likely to be of substantial
value to the defence and should be disclosed.

It is a good idea to make a checklist of questions to be asked about
unused material in cases which have any unusual features.

The question of seeking disclosure of documents from third parties has
recently become of growing importance and difficulty. It is important for
the defence advocate to have a complete working knowledge of the facts
of the case to enable an accurate formulation to be made of what is
required from, for example, Social Services, or a bank or a takeover
panel.

The Statutory Framework is the Criminal Evidence (Attendance of
Witnesses) Act 1965. A summons should be issued, at the request of the
defence, from the Crown Court at which the case is to be tried. The
summons must be carefully drafted; it must not simply seek material
which may be useful in cross-examination. If it does, the summons is
likely to be set aside under s. 2(2) of the Act, upon the recipient of the
summons asserting that he is not able to produce any evidence or thing
that is likely to be of material evidence. The request to be valid should
be designed to throw up evidence which is likely to be relevant and
admissible in the trial. For the current view on what is material see the
case of *R* v *Keane* [1994] 99 Cr App R 1.

A distinction needs also to be drawn between an application to resist
a summons on the grounds provided by s. 2(2) and, thereafter, if the
summons stands, any question which may arise on public interest
immunity.

The law is developing on this topic and this is not the place to discuss
it minutely; but I have drawn attention to it as a good illustration of how
important it is for the advocate to adapt his preparation techniques to
current developments.

It is not within the scope of this book to deal with pleadings, but it is
relevant to stress the importance of having a clear and detailed
knowledge of how you intend to present the case at the time when you

do the pleadings. It sometimes happens, for example, that you have no full proof of evidence from the plaintiff, say in a case in which a company is the plaintiff, and incorrect pleading based on insufficient information can play havoc with the presentation of the case in court.

If you intend to cite authorities, set out the order in which you wish to refer to them for your own assistance; of course have them properly flagged, and if you are in a court which is unlikely to have the authorities readily available, take an extra copy with you for the use of the court. A good photostat is adequate. This also applies to cases where a statute, or statutory instrument is unlikely to be available at court.

As you are responsible for everything to do with the presentation of the case in court, you must consider the form and contents of schedules, even if they are drawn up by someone else. Good schedules make for clear presentation and can save court time, but they often require much skill and thought in compilation, so that they are at once useful and unobjectionable.

Consideration must be given to the order in which witnesses are to be called. Often it may simply be a matter of consulting their convenience; but sometimes the order in which they are called may affect materially the cogency of the case you are presenting. Some writers on advocacy have advised that it is best to call an intelligent and plainly honest witness first (this presupposes that you have one), then witnesses who are connected with the same subject-matter in sequence, saving a good witness to the end. Suffice it to say that thought should always be given to whether there is a sound reason for calling witnesses in a particular order, and if there is, do so. It is a good cautionary rule never to call a witness whom your opponent will be compelled to call; the main reason is that this will enable you to cross-examine the witness. You should make it an inviolable rule never to call a witness 'blind'; that is to say without knowing what he is likely to say.

So as to illustrate some of the ideas which have been discussed it might be useful to give an example of the way in which each side might set about preparing a case of shoplifting. It is necessary to take simple facts by way of example, but you will be able to adapt the principles of preparation to any kind of case. The primary facts alleged are as follows.

A store detective sees a man peeling off the label on a tin of shaving cream, and immediately afterwards putting his hand into his pocket momentarily. She then sees him handling a smaller tin of the same brand, and sees him removing the label from that tin. She suspects him, but does not see him putting the cheaper label on the more expensive tin. A few minutes later she sees him apparently taking off the price label from another tin, and putting his hand into his pocket. She does not, on this occasion, see him taking a label off the small variety. Next, she gets near enough to his shopping trolley to see in the basket a large bottle of cooking oil, but notices that the price on it is that of a small bottle. The man ultimately goes to the check out, and pays for all the goods in his trolley, including the three items which the prosecution say were underpriced. The girl on the till does not query any of the prices. The man then goes out of the shop. The store detective then asks him to return with her to the shop. When the goods are examined the store detective satisfies herself that the three items are indeed underpriced, and when the police arrive, shows them the underpriced items and takes them to the shelves from which they came; and the police satisfy themselves, by looking at the containers on the shelf, that the containers bought by the defendant were underpriced. The man when asked about the underpriced items says that he did not change the labels, and that he cannot understand what has happened.

The prosecutor has these facts in his brief and is told that the only witnesses whom it is intended to call are the store detective and the police.

In the preparation of the case the first step, after grasping the essential facts, is to make a chronology of the movements of the man as observed by the store detective. No new aspect of the case emerges from this exercise, but it forms a useful aid to memory.

The first point of substance is to try to see what the issues in the case are likely to be. Is there a point of law? The count of theft is not bad for duplicity and there is no obvious point which is likely to be taken. It follows that the dispute is bound to be on the facts themselves. The defendant is obviously going to challenge the store detective on her evidence that she saw him remove the labels from two containers. This raises the question of whether there is any additional evidence that the store detective can give? Did she return to the shelves from which the goods were taken and try to find smaller containers than the ones taken, with an overpriced label, or more likely with no label at all? (Let us say that the answer to this query is that she did look but could find nothing of evidential value.) Next, did she search the man's pocket to see if there were any screwed up labels there. (Let us assume that she says that she did not search the pockets because she did not consider that she had a right to do so and the police did not do so either.)

The next question to consider is whether there is anything in the prosecution case as presented which tends to corroborate the account given by the store detective which is not likely to be in dispute. The answer is that there is. The most vital point in the prosecution case is the fact that the man bought no fewer than three items which were underpriced. There is little prospect of the defendant denying that fact, and if he did, he is unlikely to be believed. That, then is the point for the prosecution to fasten on. In opening the facts you will put that point in the forefront of your argument. It is a useful general principle to bear in mind that when you are making allegations you should pile up as many facts which lead to the conclusion of your argument; when you are defending you should seek to divide and isolate the facts alleged against you. In this instance the prosecution will say 'If there had been one item underpriced, there might have been a mistake, if there had been two items underpriced, that would have been grounds for the gravest suspicion, but three items underpriced is beyond coincidence.'

If you are prosecuting you will have reached this point in your preparation and may think that your case is reasonably sound; but you will not stop there because you will have realised that if the defence have thought out the case along the same lines they too will have concluded that this is the central point of the case. So the question to be considered next is how the defence could mount an attack on this crucial prosecution argument?

The next step is to look at the exhibits. It is astonishing how often even experienced trial advocates overlook this simple and essential part of preparation. You will be looking in particular at the stick-on price labels. Usually these labels are fiendishly difficult to get off; and the question naturally arises as to how the defendant managed it, particularly without tearing them. In addition, many shops put on price labels which are perforated, so that the label if removed comes off in bits. The object of affixing this type of label is, of course, to prevent the transfer of price labels in the way alleged. This inspection of the labels may raise a substantial doubt as to whether the defendant could have done what the store detective alleges. Let us, however, assume that the inspection is not decisive one way or the other; but doubts are thickening; the case may not be open and shut. Looking at the facts from the defendant's point of view you will look for an alternative explanation of the three underpriced items happening to be in the defendant's shopping.

A possible explanation is that there is an internal fraud operating in the shop. It may be that the underpriced labels are put onto the items by the label fixer who is part of the fraud. It may be that a certain number of goods are deliberately underpriced each day to enable certain people in the know to buy those goods cheaply. It may be that the till girl is party to the fraud. This would explain why, in this case, she did not query the underpriced items when they were put up for payment by the defendant. It would also explain why the store detective did not find any items on the shelf which were unlabelled or overpriced. It may be that the defendant on this interpretation of the facts is a party to the fraud: maybe not. But the whole complexion of the case has changed.

It is apparent from this hypothesis that it is necessary for the prosecution to set on foot an enquiry to test whether there is evidence of an internal fraud. The defence for their part would be watching to see whether the prosecution provide any evidence which either confirms or rebuts this defence.

I hope that I have said enough to show how a little careful thought can show you the way to conduct the case, avoid being taken by surprise, and concentrate on the points which really matter. The principles which should guide you in your thinking are to ask and answer these questions:

(a)   What is the central issue in the case? It is remarkable how often, even in complex cases, both civil and criminal, there is but one central issue.

(b)   What factors support the prosecution or plaintiff on the central issue and what the defence. In a civil case, for example, you would be looking very carefully at the contemporaneous documents, not only to see if they tended to support one side or the other, but also to see how they match up with the oral evidence, as it is given.

(c)   Are the exhibits consistent with the case you want to make? Take the earliest opportunity to look at them, and certainly make their inspection part of your preparation.

In the chapters on speeches and questioning, you will find further advice on aspects of preparation which relate specifically to those topics, and a summary in the final chapter.

Three

Speaking in Court

Style in its finest sense, is the last acquirement of the educated mind; it is also the most useful. It pervades the whole being. The administrator with a sense for style hates waste; the engineer with a sense for style economises his material; the artisan with a sense for style prefers good work. Style is the ultimate morality of mind. (The Aims of Education, A. N. Whitehead)

When you make any speech in court, whether it be a full scale speech, like an opening speech, or merely a submission to object to a piece of inadmissible evidence, you must have a particular purpose in mind. In an opening speech it would be to lay the facts before the tribunal and to state your reasons for saying that you are entitled to a verdict. In the submission your purpose would be to obtain the exclusion of the evidence to which you object.

As a first step to constructing a speech of any sort it is necessary to have in your mind a form in which to cast it. The Ancients divided the form of a speech into the beginning or exordium, the purpose of which was to prepare the members of the audience in such a way that they would be prepared to lend a willing ear to the rest of the speech. Next came the statement of facts or if the speaker chose, the proof. The statement of facts was intended to indicate the nature of the subject on which the judge would be called upon to give judgment. The proof followed next and was designed to show that the law as applied to the facts demonstrated that the decision should be made one way and not another. The peroration was a summary of what had gone before, artistically emphasising the favourable points and undermining those of the other side.

This is no more than a scanty summary of what the rhetoricians of old discussed and debated with endless iteration and dissension, but it will serve our purpose because it provides a simple model of the way in which a speech may effectively be constructed. I shall analyse a number of examples of speeches of different sorts in order to show the detail of how the various parts of a speech are integrated to make the whole, and shall use as our guide the classic form of a speech to which I have just referred.

As our first example let us consider a speech in the magistrates court in a case of careless driving. It is the prosecution opening. The first point to bear in mind is the nature of your tribunal. It may be a lay bench of magistrates or it may be a stipendiary, sitting alone. Your opening may be slightly different depending on which it is. If you are before the stipendiary you will keep the opening as short as possible, consistent with enabling him to understand the outline of the case you are presenting, and the defendant to know the case he has to meet. The reason for this is that a stipendiary is likely to have a long list of cases to hear and will not want to listen to a full-blown opening in which detailed facts and elementary propositions of law are elaborated. Before a lay bench, however, you may, with advantage be a little more expansive without losing effect if you have reason to think that they are inexperienced or perhaps not as quick at grasping the issues as the professional judge.

As a general rule brevity in a speech of any sort is a great virtue. It is an art difficult to acquire and is based on clarity of thought; but you may wonder what brevity in practice, as opposed to a vague exhortation, means. Quintilian deals excellently with this virtue (*loc. cit.*, Book IV 2 43.). He says:

> Personally, when I use the word brevity, I mean not saying less, but not saying more than the occasion demands. As for repetitions and tautologies and diffuseness, which some writers of text books tell us to avoid, I pass them by; they are faults we should shun for other reasons beside our desire for brevity. But we must be equally on our guard against the obscurity which results from excessive abridgement, and it is better to say a little more than a little less. We must therefore avoid even the famous terseness of Sallust (though in his case of course it is a merit), and shun all abruptness of speech, since a style which presents no difficulty to a leisurely reader, flies past a hearer and will

not stay to be looked at again; and whereas the reader is almost always a man of learning the Judge (lay Magistrate) often comes to his panel from the countryside and is expected to give his decision on what he can understand. Consequently we must aim, perhaps everywhere, but above all in our statement of facts, at striking the happy mean in our language, and the happy mean may be defined as saying just what is necessary and just what is sufficient. I mean not the bare minimum necessary to convey our meaning, for our brevity must not be devoid of elegance, without which it would merely be uncouth: pleasure beguiles the attention, and that which delights us ever seems less long, just as a picturesque and easy journey tires us less for all its length than a difficult short cut through an arid waste. And I would never carry my desire for brevity so far as to refuse admission to details which may contribute to the plausibility of the narrative. Simplify and curtail your statement of facts in every direction and you will turn it into something more like a confession. Moreover the circumstances of the case will often necessitate a long statement of facts in which case . . . the Judge should be prepared for it at the conclusion of the exordium.

You will find in Appendix 1 an example of a complete speech in a fraud case. It is a speech made by Sir Patrick Hastings for Mr Morland, an eminent chartered accountant, who was charged together with Lord Kylsant and acquitted. Sir Patrick Hastings always conducted his cases with remarkable brevity. He claimed that he seldom made a speech of more than half an hour. In recent years there has been a strong surge of feeling, certainly among the judiciary, that the long-winded style of advocacy should be replaced by a sharper, more focused and concentrated style of speaking. The European Courts, where the advocate is restricted in oral submissions to 20–30 minutes, vividly illustrates the trend. The rule of thumb when planning your speech is to see if you can omit anything which does not contribute materially to the strength of your argument or to the clarity of its presentation. More concise advocacy calls for preparation which defines what is really important in the advancement of the case you have to make; and makes you decide what you are not going to say. Rigorous pruning will always be required. But I am told by advocates who have had to make short speeches, for example at Luxembourg, that the discipline is most salutary, and sometimes they even find that in the end they have time to spare. While bearing well in mind Quintilian's warning about over-terseness, short speeches should always be aimed at; they make a more vivid impression on your tribunal than a speech which wanders along without any urgency, focus or direction.

After this long preliminary on brevity I now return to the opening by the prosecution in a careless driving case. Suppose it to be before a bench of lay magistrates in the country. The facts appear from the speech itself.

May it please you Sir, I appear for the prosecution and my learned friend Mr Snooks for the defendant.

The defendant, who has a clean driving licence, is charged with careless driving on 2 January this year. At about 2 p.m. he was driving on the road called Deepdene Avenue which you probably all know. May I hand in a sketch plan of the scene of the accident. My learned friend has no objection to your having it at this stage of the case. The circumstances of what occurred may be summarised in this way:

The defendant was driving his green Datsun along Deepdene Avenue towards the town centre. He came to that road junction which is shown in the middle of the plan. When he reached the junction the prosecution contend that he should have stopped; as you see from the plan, and will doubtless recall from your own knowledge of the junction, there is a stop sign on the approach to the junction, and appropriate road markings. It is alleged that instead of stopping, the defendant, intending to turn left, drove out into the path of a blue Rover driven by Mrs Rabbit. She had no possible chance of avoiding a collision: as she will tell you, when the defendant came out of the junction, she was no more than 15 yards away. She was doing, she will tell you, about 25 m.p.h., and certainly well within the speed limit for that stretch of road, which is 40 m.p.h. She could not avoid colliding with the rear off-side of the defendant's car. The prosecution contend that the position of the damage to the defendant's car confirms the account given by Mrs Rabbit because it is consistent with the failure by the defendant to complete the turn he intended to make to his left. The first and only thing that he said to Mrs Rabbit after the collision was 'I am sorry, I didn't see you'. When the police arrived, some ten minutes later, he said to PC Bear: 'When I drove out I had plenty of time. She must have accelerated and she was certainly driving too fast.' The prosecution say that by that time he had reflected on his position and was seeking to place the blame on Mrs Rabbit, whereas immediately after the accident he was accepting the blame.

The question which you have to decide is whether the defendant was driving with that degree of care that a reasonably prudent driver would have exercised, having regard to all the circumstances which prevailed at the time. You have, of course, to be sure of his guilt before you could find him guilty, and if you have any reasonable doubt he is entitled to be acquitted. But the prosecution say that there is no room for doubt that the defendant drove carelessly on this occasion.

Notes.

(1) The classic form of a speech has been followed. The exordium could not be briefer. It consists in the introduction of the advocate and his opponent in the time-honoured way. There is much to be said for formality and courtesy in court; it helps to keep the temperature low and to prevent personalities intruding into the presentation of a case. In this opening formula you have respect for the bench and for your opponent encompassed in one sentence. There is also one further touch in this opening which falls within the purpose of the exordium. It is the reference to the defendant's clean licence, at the earliest possible moment. It is scrupulously fair, as befits a prosecution advocate who is a Minister of Justice, whose duty it is to place before the court anything which he knows to be favourable to the accused. Mentioning good character immediately has the collateral effect of demonstrating to the bench that the advocate lives up to the necessary standards of fairness and can be trusted. This is, perhaps, an example of the way in which advocacy operates at more than one level. Probably not one in a hundred listening to this speech would say to himself 'This advocate has satisfied me that he is fair', but most would feel that he was without thinking about it.

(2) Almost immediately the speaker turns to the statement of facts. It is essential to make the statement of facts clear and as interesting as the facts allow. By referring to the possibility that the bench themselves know the place where the accident happened he at once makes them personally involved in following the narrative. Perhaps one of the bench came that way that morning. He will visualise the scene and be able to help his colleagues when they retire.

(3) One of the characteristics of this opening is that it anticipates the evidence which will be called in some detail. For example, there is the reference to the green Datsun and the blue Rover. This is because he knows that a witness to the collision will refer to the cars by their colour only. But he has deliberately omitted any reference to the witness because his evidence is vague and inconclusive and he does not want to rely on it to substantiate his case; and yet, on the other hand, he thinks that he should in fairness to the defence call him to give evidence.

(4)   In a case like this it is important to provide, at least, a sketch plan of the scene of the accident. There is nothing more irritating to a listener, who does not know the area to be told that the accident occurred to the west of point A and to the south east of point B without having the remotest idea of what is being described.

(5)   It is part of his argument to show that the defendant was enjoined by the signs on the road to stop and that if he did not stop he cannot excuse himself. The speaker has evidently thought out what the defence may be; namely that the defendant did stop. The defendant may say that he looked to his right and the road was clear. He emerged slowly and carefully, but the collision occurred because the other car was being driven at speed, and had come up round the bend, 50 yards away from the junction, far too fast. In contrast the other driver is evidently saying that she was driving properly and the accident was entirely the defendant's fault. You should observe that the advocate does not make the general assertion that the other driver was 'driving properly' but spells out the details of her proper driving. This is a basic principle of good exposition, but care should be given to include only those details which are necessary to carry conviction; do not overload your statement with profuse detail. As Mao Tse Tung put it, 'Don't overload your chopsticks or you will get rice up your nose.'

(6)   In a case like this you will have thought out the issues which are likely to arise in your preparation. As he is pleading not guilty, you may first ask yourself: Is he relying on a point of law? That looks very unlikely because there is no doubt that he was required by the signs to stop before emerging from the junction, but you should check that there is not a technical point on road signs. Had, for example, the stop sign blown down?

Assuming that there is no such technical argument available, the likely defence must be on the facts. He will, therefore, be disputing the other driver's account. What are the vulnerable points in her account? If you have visited the scene of the accident you will have noticed that there is a bend some 50 yards from the junction. If the Rover was driven at a high speed it is possible that the defendant could have stopped at the junction, seen that nothing was coming, and was making his turn when the other car, coming so fast, could not stop before the collision. Furthermore, the defendant may say that what he said was, 'I'm sorry, but I did not see you because you were driving so fast.' If such a defence is foreseen it is likely that you will have advised that expert evidence should be called to say whether the extent of the damage would tend to confirm one account rather than the other and this will be the determining evidence in the case. If you had such evidence available you would, of course, include it in your opening. From this analysis you will see how careful thought about the implications of the facts can enable you to see exactly how the case is likely to unfold. You are then in a position to frame your opening to cope with the possible defence.

In the example the advocate has opened the prosecution case strongly on the account given by the Rover driver. She was going at 25 m.p.h., well within the speed limit. She was only 15 yards away when she saw the defendant emerge: the position of the damage confirms her account. The defendant's alleged remark makes it appear that he was accepting the blame; and the argument is advanced that he changed his account on reflection. All these alleged facts are spelt out in necessary detail and give the impression of an unanswerable case. The purpose is to get your case firmly into the minds of the magistrates.

It might be said, in criticism of this opening, that it runs the risk that the driver of the Rover will not come up to proof; if that happens the case is certain to fail, whereas if it had not been opened so high it might have been possible to rely on the weaker version of what happened. In a criminal case, there is much to be said for this view when it is expressed as a general rule. Criminal cases, if they are soundly based, usually get stronger as they progress and particularly when the defendant gives evidence. It is, therefore, wise to open the case low and in that way you avoid the risk that your witnesses will say much less than you expect. While this is generally a good rule to follow in criminal prosecutions, it does not apply with nearly the same force to civil cases. The reason is that in a civil case where you are opening for the plaintiff, you will have had an opportunity of appraising for yourself, the likelihood of the plaintiff saying what you expect him to say because you are able to see him in conference and take instructions directly from him, whereas you may not do so with a witness for the prosecution.

I think that in the illustration, I would open in the way suggested notwithstanding the possible criticism because in this instance the case stands or falls on the evidence of this witness if no expert evidence is available.

(7)   After the statement of facts comes the proof. At first glance it might appear that the formulation of the point to be decided is a little stiffly worded, but in fact it is a very precise statement of the relevant law, taken from *Simpson* v *Peat* [1954] 2 QB 24. There is much virtue in encapsulating the relevant law into your opening speech, which can be

readily understood and referred to by the court as the focal point of the case as it progresses.

(8)   The peroration or summary is necessarily very short in this case and it neatly rounds off the speech.

The principles which emerge from this analysis may be summarised as follows:

(a)   Put yourself on good terms with the court.

(b)   State the facts of the case plainly.

(c)   Pace yourself so that you are sure that the court is following what you are saying (production of the plan).

(d)   Spell out your argument by referring to the facts on which it is based.

(e)   Present a word-picture in which the thing described is vivid to the mind's eye. Don't merely say 'She couldn't avoid the accident'; say rather, 'When the defendant unexpectedly came out of the junction she was no more than 15 yards away; there was a car coming in the opposite direction so she could not swerve to the right; there was a line of trees on her nearside so she could not swerve to the left; the only thing she could do was to slam on the brakes and hope.'

(f)   State the law as simply and accurately as you can.

(g)   Anticipate, as far as you can, your opponent's case and construct your speech accordingly.

The next example to look at is the short speech by way of interjection. It is often necessary, in every type of case, to deal with a point as it arises on the spur of the moment. A typical example is where you wish to object to some piece of evidence. Suppose your opponent has asked a witness-in-chief, 'Now don't tell us what was said, but did you speak to the man and as a result do something else'. As soon as you hear this question coming, and you want to object to it, you should say 'No' as you rise to your feet. This immediately stops the question and prevents the damage being done. Once you are on your feet, you might say something along these lines: 'I'm sorry to interrupt my friend, but the question is a plain attempt to get round the hearsay rule; if I need authority, I rely on what Lord Devlin said in *Glinsky* v *McIvor*. I particularly ask my friend not to lead hearsay evidence by the front or the back door.'

Notes.

(1) By apologising you are explaining to the judge and your opponent that you would not be interrupting unless it was necessary to do so. I recall an occasion when I made this very objection and was immediately told to sit down by the judge, who until the authority was cited to him, thought that my objection was not only unfounded but impertinent.

(2) In a few words the point of the objection has been formulated in clear terms. It is equivalent to the statement of facts.

(3) The proof is contained in the citation of the authority. It is an inestimable advantage if you have the rules of evidence and authorities to support critical propositions in your head.

(4) The objection is neatly rounded-off by a courteous rebuke. There has been no blustering, perfect good manners have been observed and yet you have made your point firmly, and in this case, unanswerably.

This kind of effective interjection depends on promptitude of mind, which in turn depends on knowing the proper basis on which to found the objection. When you are starting advocacy you may think that being prompt and ready for such spontaneous speech will take years to achieve. Obviously the more you are in court the easier it will become; but the fact is that you can, to a great extent, prepare for this kind of point. You see some important point as likely to come up in the course of the case, and you consider it from every angle. Can you exclude it? How could the other side try to get it in evidence? What riposte would you have if he did try?

The next example to consider is a submission on a point of law. The example is taken from *R* v *Manchester Stipendiary Magistrate, Ex parte Hill* [1983] AC 328. The question to be considered was what constitutes a laying of an information for the purposes of s. 127 of the Magistrates' Courts Act 1980?

Suppose that you wanted to interest the Appeal Committee of the House of Lords in the point so that they would grant you leave to appeal. You might do it along these lines:

'The point raised by the proposed appeal is whether an information is laid at the time when it is laid before and considered, by a justice of the peace (or the clerk to the justices) under the Justices Clerks Rules 1970, or alternatively whether it is laid when it is received at the office of the clerk to the justices by a member of the staff expressly or impliedly authorised to receive it. It is a point of great practical importance to the proper administration of justice because of the great volume of work which has to be undertaken by justices and the clerks to justices.

For hundreds of years before *Reg.* v *Gateshead Justices, Ex parte Tesco Stores Ltd* [1981] QB 470, it was accepted that an information was laid when it was delivered at Court; but in *Gateshead* it was held that an information was not 'laid before a justice of the peace' for the purposes of the Magistrates Courts Act 1980 s. 127 unless it was laid before and considered by a justice or the clerk to the justices under the Justices Clerks Rules 1970.

It is submitted that *Gateshead* contains a basic fallacy in that it confuses the stage of laying the information and the stage of issuing the summons. It is surprising that *Gateshead* was not brought to your Lordships' House for consideration, but the opportunity to consider the point has arisen in this case.

Our submission is that there is no reason in principle why the practice before *Gateshead* should not be continued and there are the practical reasons of the saving of time and expense in the administration of justice to recommend the view that *Gateshead* should be overruled.'

Notes.

(1)   The purpose of this little speech is to satisfy the court that there is a point of principle of practical importance to be decided and that the opportunity of considering the point should not be allowed to slip by.

(2)   The aim should be to seize the court's attention immediately. This can best be done by formulating the point at issue without preliminaries; and great care has been taken to state the point succinctly and accurately. Succinctly because the House of Lords, of all courts, is likely to be irritated by verbiage, and accurately because they will be acute to spot any loose-thinking.

(3)   Next, the practical importance of the point is mentioned to stimulate the interest of the court, so that they appreciate at once that it is not a merely academic question.

(4)   A contrast is made between hundreds of years when the practice remained unchallenged and the aberrant decision in *Gateshead*.

Antithetical statement is a very useful device for highlighting points and giving them a startling clarity; but you should be discriminating in its use. Lord Macaulay used it exorbitantly; as a result he never wrote obscurely, and yet, on the other hand, Mathew Arnold said that it was impossible to tell the truth with a style like that.

(5)   The point is boldly taken that *Gateshead* was wrongly decided. There is no advantage in putting the point with your position hedged by 'it might be said', 'there are some grounds for saying that' and the like. The important thing is to found a bold submission on a formidable argument, and to state the argument in clear terms. When you attack a strong authority, remember the maxim 'if you strike at a King, you must kill him'.

(6)   The summary is an effective appeal to the court to give leave to appeal. It should be noted that the argument thus presented is a flowing whole. It is a cohesive argument presented in a logical form and is the result of distilling the facts and competing arguments to bare essentials, as you will see if you look at the decision itself.

As a last example let me take an opening speech in the county court on a boundary dispute. This is the kind of case where a full, detailed, and strong opening is required. As usual, clarity of statement is essential; with this regard you should always remember that you have studied the case, you have the facts and the law applicable to them, teeming in your mind. The judge may not even have seen the papers before you begin your opening. You should not assume that the judge knows anything of the subject-matter of your case, but you should also be very careful not to explain the self-evident. It is a difficult balance to achieve. It is, I suppose, largely a matter of feel; minutely observing the judge's response to what you are saying is a sure guide. Once you sense that you are descending into too much detail, or amplifying a point which has already been taken, you should be flexible enough to break off gracefully and turn to something new. There are many situations which arise frequently in every sort of case where it is useful to have a neat way of expressing the transition from one point to another. Francis Bacon in *The Advancement of Learning* has this to say: 'For as in buildings there is a great pleasure and use in the well casting of the staircases, entries, doors, windows and the like; so in speech, the conveyances and passages are of special ornament and effect.' Bacon recommends that the speaker should equip himself beforehand with antitheses and formulae; that is, sentences and phrases that are needed for different kinds of opening, conclusions, links, transitions, repartees etc. (In his *Promus of Formularies and Elegancies* (ed. Mrs Henry Pott, 1883) he has made a collection of them.)

You begin your opening by introducing the parties to the dispute; followed by a statement of the points at issue. This is of fundamental importance so that the judge can refer to the rival contentions as the case unfolds. I emphasise this because I have so often heard advocates who launch into the facts of the case without troubling to explain what the issues are and how they arose. This fault can so easily be avoided if you ask yourself in preparation how you can express what the case is about so simply that a child could understand.

The next stage is to explain the detailed facts of the land in dispute. Invariably in this class of case you will need to explain to the court the lie of the land with the aid of scale plans. Make sure that you yourself understand them perfectly. It can ruin the smooth presentation of the case if you are asked a question by the judge and have to say 'I'm sorry, I'll have to take instructions.' If you have any say in the way in which the plans are drawn up, you should specify that they should be of manageable size. There is often inadequate space on the judge's desk, and if the plans are numerous and awkward to handle, the judge may become irritable and unable to follow what you are saying as you would wish. This is a simple example of the psychology of advocacy, about which I shall have a little more to say further on.

When you have explained the lie of the land you next explain in detail the rival contentions. This is your opportunity to present your case in a favourable light and it should be used as skilfully as possible; but in dealing with your opponent's case it is imperative that you should state it accurately and fairly. This is a principle of debate. If you can express the opposite view as strongly as it can be put, and then demolish it with the weight of your own argument you will be more convincing than you would be if you merely presented your own argument.

Finally it may be necessary to deal in detail with the law applicable to the case. Sometimes it will only be necessary to touch on it in your opening; at other times, when it will place your case in a more favourable light, or perhaps place a difficulty in the way of your opponent, you will want to deal with it thoroughly.

In making a defence speech it is often a problem to decide whether it is better to try to deal with the points made by the other side, or to make your own points without specific reference to the argument of your opponent. That is the way in which the problem often seems to present itself when you begin to think about how you will reply to the other side. The problem is not so simple or clear-cut as that. But the short answer to be given to the question is that you should not answer the points made by the other side one by one in the order in which they were presented. They were presented in that way, if done artistically, so as to give the greatest force to the argument. You must do likewise in presenting your own argument. Certainly deal with the points made against you; it would be foolish not to, unless you have no answer that will bear examination. But make your answer a consistent, flowing whole; and deal with your opponent's points within the texture of your own argument. Because your argument is freestanding, when you answer your opponent the tenor of the whole argument lends support to the separate points which make up the whole.

While much has been said about the importance of clarity in speaking, next to nothing has been said, up to now, about useful ornament. The question arises as to whether tropes and figures of speech and thought should be used in everyday speaking in the courts, and if so, how it should be done. It is, I believe, this aspect of speaking that is in the main responsible for giving rhetoric a bad name; this is because when ornament is attempted in speaking it is often done badly. The effect is one of insincerity in the speaker, and the audience is left with the feeling that their intelligence has been affronted by an attempt to play upon their goodwill. It is the part of good speaking, first and foremost, to avoid error. As Quintilian puts it (*loc. cit.*, Book VIII 3 42): 'Before I discuss ornament, I must first touch upon its opposite, since the first of all virtues is the avoidance of faults. Therefore we must not expect any speech to be ornate that is not, in the first place, acceptable.'

The fundamental rule which enables you to use the ornaments of speech with the purpose of enhancing your presentation to the delight of your hearers is to make your language spring from your subject-matter. The opposite is to seize upon florid language and try to make it express what you want to say: the result is inevitably artificial, inimical to truth, false in feeling, and unfaithful to what is meant. Let me illustrate this. Here is the imaginary peroration by Mr Florid in a shop-lifting case:

Members of the jury, the defendant, my client, whom I have the honour to represent, stands before you charged with an iniquitous offence. There may be good honest decent shopkeepers who will feel appalled by the wickedness which is alleged against my client. He is charged with shoplifting; but if he were to have been charged with genocide he would have been entitled to a fair trial at your hands, you are the bulwarks of liberty, you stand as juries have always stood, between the state and the individual; and in your hands reposes the reputation of the defendant. As Shakespeare said 'Reputation reputation reputation! O! I have lost my reputation. I have lost the immortal part of myself, and what remains is bestial'.

In this case members of the jury, if you have a scintilla of doubt about the guilt of the accused you must do your duty. After all England expects every man and woman to do his or her duty: I beg you members of the jury to say to yourselves 'There but for the Grace of God go I'; and acquit my client.

I have incorporated in Mr Florid's peroration some of the sentiments and quotations that I have over the years heard thrust into such a speech. I intend by this illustration to warn against inappropriate language, quotation and sentiment. Compare this with Norman Birkett's final words in the Mancini murder trial (*Norman Birkett* by Montgomery Hyde, Reprint Society, 1965, p. 416):

Defending Counsel has a most solemn duty, as I and my colleagues know only too well. We have endeavoured, doubtless with many imperfections, to perform that task to the best of our ability. The ultimate responsibility, that rests upon you — and never let it be said, never let it be thought, that any word of mine should seek to deter you from doing that which you feel to be your duty. But now that the whole of the matter is before you, I think I am entitled to claim for this man a verdict of not guilty. And, members of the jury, in returning that verdict, you will vindicate a principle of law, that people are not tried by newspapers, not tried by rumour, but tried by juries called to do justice and to decide upon the evidence. I ask you for, I appeal to you for, and I claim from you, a verdict of not guilty.

His biographer says: '... he stopped as if about to sit down. But he remained on his feet for a few moments longer, during which time he allowed his eyes to rove up and down the jury box. Then his voice rang out, as he gave the jury a last admonition ''Stand firm''.'

The characteristic of this passage is that it was entirely appropriate to the circumstances of the case and arose naturally from them and that the final admonition was a product of the tension and drama which had been created by what had gone before.

Use metaphor, simile, figures of speech and all the rest freely, if, but only if, you can do it naturally and appropriately. I think that the best way of learning how to do it, is to read widely in English literature and see how it has been done in former times. I cannot resist quoting, as a perfect example of apt metaphor, a passage from Francis Bacon's preface to his biography of Henry VII addressed to the Prince of Wales: 'For he was a wise man, and an excellent King; and yet the times were rough and full of mutations and rare accidents. And it is with times as it is with ways: some are more up hill and down hill, and some are more flat and plain; and the one is better for the liver, and the other for the writer. I have not flattered him, but took him to life, sitting so far off and having no better light.'

Of advocacy in the Courts there are no finer examples of persuasive speech than the speeches of Thomas Erskine (published in 5 vols by J. Ridgeway, 1810), Henry Brougham (*Essays*, vol. I p. 57, Richard Griffin and Co., 1856) says of Erskine's speech for Stockdale: 'Mr Erskine then delivered the finest of all his orations — whether we regard the wonderful skill with which the argument is conducted, — the soundness of the principles laid down, and their happy application to the case, — or the exquisite fancy with which they are embellished and illustrated, — and the powerful and touching language in which they are conveyed. It is justly regarded, by all English lawyers, as a consummate specimen of the art of addressing a jury: as a standard, a sort of precedent for treating cases of libel, by keeping which, in his eye a man might hope to succeed in special pleading . . .'. Erskine's language is, needless to say, of an age that has passed, but just as we may learn from the structure of Burke's writings, so also can we learn from Erskine. On reading his speeches what is particularly obvious is his ability to focus on the fundamental points in issue; to argue closely on the facts, to express his arguments in the most telling language which, for all its power of imagery and imagination, never for a moment is parted from the theme of the argument: and he never indulges in a flight of oratory which is not strictly designed to place his argument in a better light. He exemplified Quintilian's maxim that '. . . our aim must be not to put the judge in a position to understand our argument, but to force him to understand it' (*loc. cit.*, Book VIII 2 24).

At this point I think it useful to consider some examples of submissions which might be made in the course of proceedings. A submission should be constructed in the same way as a full-blown speech. It should be presented in clear and simple language. It should state the point at issue at the outset and the law which is relevant to the decision which has to be made. The art is to present a compelling view of the facts and law which lead to the conclusion for which you contend. Do not forget that it is the role of the advocates to advance competing arguments to the Court; and it is for the Judge to choose between them. That is sometimes forgotten by some advocates; there are occasions when it seems that an advocate has himself decided the issue, and as a result the presentation of the argument is lifeless. The wise words of Dr Johnson are apposite; 'Sir, a lawyer has no business with the justice or injustice of the cause which he undertakes, unless the client asks his opinion, and then he is bound to give it honestly. The justice or injustice of the cause is to be decided by the judge. Consider, Sir, what is the purpose of courts of justice? It is that every man shall have his case fairly tried by men appointed to try causes ... a lawyer is not to usurp the province of the jury or judge and determine what shall be the effect of the evidence or the result of legal argument ... if lawyers were to undertake no such causes until they were sure that they were just, a man might be precluded altogether from a trial of his claim, though if it were judicially examined it might be found a very just claim.'

Now take some specific submissions which may occur in criminal or civil proceedings.

Criminal Law
It often happens that the young barrister, just starting practice, may be asked to make an application, on behalf of a more senior member of chambers, to have a case fixed for hearing taken out of the list. The reasons for the application may be that an expert witness is not available and that the defendant's counsel of choice is not available.

Your approach to the preparation of your submissions should be to define clearly what your objectives are. Do you want to defer the trial date for a day or two to accommodate the expert and counsel, or do you seek a much longer adjournment? If the latter, you will have to consider carefully what effect the adjournment is likely to have, for example on co-defendants, or on the defendant himself who may be in custody. What effect will it have on witnesses: perhaps it is a case where children are giving evidence and they have already been warned to attend on the fixture date. (The judge is likely to be unwilling to defer the hearing in such a case unless there are very cogent reasons for doing so.)

May it please your Honour, I make this application on behalf of the first defendant to vacate the fixture of 21 June and to defer the start of the case to the Monday of the following week. Since the fixture was made some three months ago, two unforeseen events have occurred, and both those events have been beyond the control of the Defendant or his legal advisers. Three days ago my Instructing Solicitors received a letter from Dr Moriarty, to say that there was a high likelihood that in the week beginning 21 June he would still be giving evidence in the

High Court; and that he could not guarantee his availability until the following Monday, 28 June. As your Honour will know the evidence of the Doctor is central to the case for the Defence; and it is highly desirable if not essential, for him to be in court during the prosecution case so that he can assess the degree to which the circumstantial detail described by the scientific witnesses supports or undermines the case for the prosecution.

The second event that has occurred is that counsel leading for the defence will not be available now until Friday 25 June because the case in which he is currently engaged has overrun its estimate by five weeks.

I have discussed this application with my learned friends for the prosecution and those who represent the second defendants and while not supporting the application they do not oppose it. Please may I ask your Honour to defer the start of the case for one week.

Notes.

(1)   The limited objective of the application is stated immediately.

(2)   In such applications the judge will inevitably want to know why the original date for the hearing was fixed with the approval of the applicant if he now wants to vacate it. The point is dealt with at the outset by implication.

(3)   The whole tenor of the submission is restrained and reasoned; it also takes account of the attitude of the other parties.

(4)   The better point is advanced first and presented in a way which implies that an injustice may well be done to the defendant if the vital witness is not present for the first week of the trial; but the point is not overstated.

(5)   The language in which the submission is couched is clear and without any kind of 'flannel'.

Civil Law

Take for our example an application for an injunction to restrain the defendant from blocking the plaintiff's access to the road. The access way is the subject of a boundary dispute between the plaintiff and the defendant. A problem which often puzzles the beginner is how to refer to such well-known authorities as the *American Cyanamid* case without irritating the judge who may be presumed to have heard of it.

May it please your Honour, I appear for the Plaintiff and my learned friend Miss Jones appears for the Defendant. This is an application by the Plaintiff for an injunction to restrain the Defendant from blocking with his tractor the access way from the Plaintiff's house to the main road. The access way is the land in dispute in the action. May I refer your Honour to the plan marked A which will be found on the first page of the bundle of documents. Your Honour will see that the access way lies to the right of the Plaintiff's land, as you look at the plan; and to the left of the Defendant's land. May I also refer your Honour to the conveyance of the property to the Plaintiff from his predecessor in title. The Plaintiff contends that the access way formed part of the conveyance to him, and he has been using it for many years without any let or hindrance from anybody. But the Defendant now contends that the right of way either wholly or in part belongs to him.

The first point on which I must satisfy your Honour is whether there is a serious issue to be tried. It is my contention that there clearly is a serious issue to be tried since there is a substantial dispute between the Plaintiff and the Defendant over the access. It is a mixed question of law and fact. The issues are plainly set out in the pleadings. May I refer your Honour to them at pages 7–12 of the blue bundle.

Your Honour will see that there can be little dispute that there is a serious and substantial issue to try.

If your Honour is satisfied about that, your Honour will in deciding whether or not to grant the injunction, have to weigh up in whose favour the balance of convenience lies.

The Defendant's action in blocking the access with his tractor, is a substantial nuisance to the Plaintiff, even though he has an alternative route to the road. At the present time it is flooded and in a wet summer does not dry out. The damage which the plaintiff is suffering is non-pecuniary. Damages in this case would therefore not be an adequate remedy. If I may refer your Honour to the draft minutes of order at page 7 of the white bundle, your Honour will see that the Plaintiff gives an undertaking in damages.

It is my submission that there is no reason for not granting the injunction which the Plaintiff seeks unless to do so would cause the Defendant injury which cannot be compensated by damages. If your Honour looks at the Defendant's affidavit you will see that there is no suggestion that he could not be compensated in damages if the injunction were to be granted.

I therefore assert that the balance of convenience is heavily weighted in the Plaintiff's favour. I therefore submit that the injunction the Plaintiff seeks should be granted in the terms of the draft order.

Notes.

(1)   The legal framework of the submission is made tacitly without specific mention of the *American Cyanamid* case; and yet the principles which that case lays down are referred to specifically. Is there a triable issue? If so, where does the balance of convenience lie?

(2)   The facts are arranged so as to fit into the legal framework. The impression which is conveyed is that everything which is said is relevant to the decision which has to be made.

(3)   The argument is logically arranged and there is no danger of the Judge losing his way. The submission is well paced and enables the judge to follow what is being said without difficulty. (Note the reference to the plan and the layout simply described and to the relevant documents as the argument advances.)

(4)   The brevity of the application is achieved by paring the argument down to what really matters. There may, for example, be other, less cogent, reasons for saying that the balance of convenience lies with the Plaintiff. But when you have an overwhelming reason, why clutter it up with make weights? It can scarcely be over-emphasised that a plain argument attractively presented in a compelling form is an essential part of effective advocacy.

Before concluding this chapter something needs to be said about the psychology of speaking. Lord Macmillan in his *Law and Other Things*, Cambridge University Press, 1937, has this to say:

The problems of pleading are all problems of psychology. One mind is working on another mind at every point and all the time. The judicial mind is subject to the laws of psychology like any other mind. When a judge assumes the ermine he does not divest himself of humanity ... the judge's mind remains a human instrument working as do other minds, though no doubt on specialised lines, and often characterised by individual traits of personality, engaging or the reverse. It is well, therefore, for the advocate not only to know his case but to know his judge in the sense of knowing the type of mind with which he has to deal ... one of the most conspicuous, and perhaps one of the most creditable of the instincts of all intellectual minds is a tendency to assist anyone who confesses he is struggling with a difficulty. I call it the instinct of rescue. There are occasions when it is worth enlisting on your side. When you know that your case is confronted with a serious difficulty in the shape of an awkward passage in the evidence or an embarrassing precedent, do not shirk it. Read the awkward passage with all emphasis or quote the authority without flinching, and point out the difficulty it creates for you. You will almost invariably find that the first instinct of the judge is to assist you by pointing out that the evidence is less damaging to you than you represented or that the precedent upon examination is distinguishable. The Court is favourably disposed by the absence of all concealment of the difficulty and is attracted by the very statement of the difficulty to address itself to the task of solving or alleviating it ... a solution which the judge himself finds for the problem ... is always of much more value to the advocate than one which he himself offers to the Court. [He adds a cautionary note.] ... The expedient of disarming your opponent by anticipating him is one to be used with discretion; it is not always possible to adopt it, nor is it always desirable to resort to it. Circumstances alter cases. Nor is it always well to dwell too emphatically on your bad points — you may defeat your object by satisfying the judge that they really are fatal to you.

All this is well said and any experienced advocate would be able to give instance after instance of the utility of this advice.

Much in advocacy depends on winning both the understanding and the sympathy of your tribunal to your case. It often happens that confrontational language will alienate that sympathy and possibly cloud the understanding with prejudice. You may avoid bitterness by using wit and humour to make your point rather than invective. There is nothing so good as the apt witticism for dissolving tension and misunderstanding, but great care should be used to be sure that you can carry it off. Experience is the only guide here; save only that you should distinguish between genuine humour and flippancy; cultivate the one and shun the other.

Four

Pleading in Mitigation

He that gives reason for what he saith has done what is fit to be done and the most that can be done. He that gives not reason speaks nothing, though he saith never so much. (Aphorism of Benjamin Whichcote, 1609-83.)

A good plea in mitigation should make the Judge feel intellectually uncomfortable if he rejects the advocate's argument.

This definition of a good plea is intended to draw attention to two particular points. The first is that you should take care to base your submissions on a realistic appraisal of the sentencing options; and secondly that you must address a cogent argument to the judge, and not a series of assertions unsupported by reasons. If you do both of these things the judge will have to wrestle with your argument and your realism before he can replace it with an argument of his own.

Good preparation is, as usual, the foundation of success. You should begin your preparation by grasping the facts of the case as alleged by the prosecution in the statements or depositions. I suggest that you should read these first, before reading the defence instructions and statements because this will prevent your sympathies being engaged before you have had a cool look at the facts against you.

Next read your instructions and the defence statements, noting particularly the points in the prosecution case which are satisfactorily explained, and no less important, those which are not. You will find that, with a little experience, the form which the mitigation should take will begin to emerge at this first reading.

You should then consider the sentencing principles which might apply to the case. *The Encyclopaedia of Current Sentencing Practice* by D. Thomas, will be an invaluable aid both in preparation and in court. It sets out all the statutory provisions on sentencing together with the guideline cases which, in the last few years, have been handed down by the Court of Appeal with increasing regularity. All the judges have and use the Encyclopaedia, so you know that if you want to cite a principle of sentencing from it, the judge will have it at his elbow.

It is the same with a speech in mitigation as it is with any other type of speech in court: you are seeking to advance a compelling argument on which you intend the judge to act. Once you have the facts of the case clearly in mind, together with the relevant principles of sentencing, you are ready to formulate your argument.

Let us look at some examples of the way in which you might approach the construction of your argument based on principle.

Suppose a man of bad character is charged with an attempt, indecently to assault a girl aged 12 years. He admits that he had an intention to assault her and that he had tried to persuade her to accompany him into a wood, but while he was trying to persuade her, not by force, he saw a police car in the distance and allowed the girl to leave.

There are two sentencing principles which clearly apply to this case. First the necessity to protect the public from such offenders; and secondly the general principle that an attempt to commit an offence ought not to carry as heavy a sentence as that for the completed offence.

If the offence had been tried a few years ago, when the maximum sentence for indecent assault on a girl of this age was five years, you would have had to bear in mind also that the maximum sentence should be reserved for the worst instance of the type of offence which is likely to occur.

The mitigation should accommodate these principles in a realistic way. The argument might run as follows. The maximum sentence for the worst example of the complete offence which is likely to occur is five years. This was an attempt only and there is no evidence that force was used or was likely to be used and therefore was not in the 'worst instance' category. He has pleaded guilty and is on authority entitled to a discount in his sentence on that ground alone, particularly as he has, by his plea, saved the girl from the ordeal of giving evidence. Despite the need to protect the public from the defendant, the appropriate sentence should be substantially below the maximum sentence of five years.

In this example no reference has been made to personal factors which might well be advanced in mitigation, and no attempt has been made to deal with the detailed facts of the case. If there are mitigating circumstances, either in the facts of the case, or personal to the offender they should be used to support or illustrate a point of principle which is being relied on in the argument. If, for example, the defendant since the offence had contracted some illness which would reduce or remove the risk of his offending similarly again, that fact could be used to negate the principle that it is necessary to pass a sentence to deter him from repeating this type of crime.

You should always be wary of advancing some fact personal to the defendant without checking to see that it is fact and not fiction. In the example just given, you would not put the point forward unless you had medical evidence, at least in the form of a letter or report, which substantiated it. In desperation a defendant will often state as a fact something which he wishes were true, little realising that if it is shown to be untrue it may damage his mitigation irreparably.

It is often unwise to try to deal with the detailed facts of the case if to do so is likely to invite awkward questions, the answers to which would not advance your case. Suppose your instructions in our example were that the defendant was walking on the heath and met the girl by chance, and that she asked him the time and that the offence occurred from that innocent beginning. The point which could be made in favour of the defendant on this account is that the offence was not premeditated; but you would have to examine the facts with great care in conference before relying on the defendant's assertion that it started innocently. Why was he walking on the heath? Did he do so often? Had he seen the girl there before? Did he go there that day hoping to see her? Had he in fact planned to lure her into the wood if the chance arose?

You will see easily whether the answers to such questions would make it dangerous to raise the supposedly chance meeting as a point in mitigation. What is required is careful thought, noting vulnerable points which if proved could undermine what at first glance appear to be valid arguments.

In sounding this cautionary note I am not saying that important facts should be omitted just because they are awkward. Suppose, in our example, the defendant had previous convictions for indecent assault and rape: it would be mere foolishness to pass them by as though they did not exist. You must deal with them as best you can because they are facts which are already in the judge's mind to weigh and consider. Such facts must be dealt with and extenuated as far as possible. You must use your own good judgment in deciding whether a point is worth making or whether the downside is too risky. In the illustration it would be too dangerous to deal with the facts on the basis of a chance meeting unless you had satisfactory answers to the questions about it in conference.

You will notice that there is no need to deal with the detail if you chose not to use it. And yet, on the other hand, you should be prepared to deal with it if the judge himself raises it. In this case, if it was the fact that the offence was planned, the Judge will give additional weight to the principle of the public's need for protection; but you would point out that the principles of sentencing on which the defence primarily stands are unaffected, and of course, there may be some other facts particular to the case that you might be able to use to counter the adverse point. Lord Baden-Powell's motto, 'Be Prepared', should be the advocate's motto too.

In contrast to the formulation of a coherent argument which I am suggesting should always be used, there are many who are content to divide a plea in mitigation into compartments, and prepare and deliver the plea in that format: antecedents; the facts of the case; and what ought to be done. Those who use this construction would say in its justification that it has the merit of simplicity: that all you have to do is to use your common sense as to the order in which you deal with each compartment and that your experience will guide you in deciding what to include in, or exclude from, any particular compartment.

There is something to be said for this arrangement of your materials, but I think, not much. To the beginner it seems attractive because you can readily see how any particular case can be presented in such compartments. Taking our illustration again, a typical, though slightly parodied presentation in this style of mitigation might go as follows.

He is aged 42. He had an unhappy childhood. His father was a drunkard. His mother died when he was 10 years old. He was himself sexually abused by his uncle with whom he lived when his mother died. He had very little love in his childhood and did not know what it was to be cared for like a normal child. He started committing offences of theft and burglary before he was 20, and during the next 10 years he committed three indecent assaults and one rape. It is to his credit that he always pleaded guilty to those offences as he has pleaded guilty today. He deserves credit for that. When he committed this offence he was very depressed because he had his wallet stolen and he had very little money to live on for the coming week. Although he is married he has not seen his wife for many years. The last occasion was in the underground at Tooting.

Turning to the facts of this sad case, he was walking on the heath, thinking about the loss of his wallet when the victim came up to him and asked the time. Nothing was further from his mind at that moment than the commission of this very serious offence. She said that he was looking rather sad that day and they began to talk together as they walked along. The defendant, who is a very unhappy man, was touched by the interest which the girl was showing in him, and it was only then, as he freely and candidly admits, that he formed the intention of taking her into the woods in the hope that he could, without using force, indecently assault her. Fortunately, at about this point the defendant saw a police car in the distance; and he realised the seriousness of what he intended to do. He told the girl not to tell anybody what he had been saying to her and hurried off; but the girl to her credit waved the car down and told the police what had happened and they arrested him a few minutes later. It is much to the defendant's credit that he confessed immediately and has pleaded guilty today and he deserves credit for that.

He is very sorry for what he has done, and tells me that he will not do it again. He thinks that the only reason why he did it this time was because he was at a low ebb having lost his wallet. The court should bear in mind that he has pleaded guilty to an attempt and has saved this little girl from having to come and give evidence. He tells me that since the offence he has lost interest in sex and thinks that it may have something to do with an illness he got while he was in Africa five years ago. When he first got this illness he says that he had no libido at all; and when he had another bout of it last month the same thing happened. I therefore urge the court to take the view that this type of offence will not be commited by this man again. Although this is a very serious offence I hope the court will bear in mind all these points in mitigation and pass as lenient a sentence as possible in all the circumstances.

Leaving aside the elements of parody which are intended to highlight the defects of this style of mitigation (which can be heard every day in the courts) the following criticisms can be made of the construction of it:

(a)   The first two compartments, background and facts, are almost entirely irrelevant to the question of what sentence should be passed. It is true that some of the facts dealt with by a series of assertions, might possibly be used in a reasoned argument, but no such argument is advanced within or outside the compartments.

(b)   The final section dealing with what sentence should be passed contains the basic material on which a good argument can be based, as we have already seen. But the material is almost completely buried by a lot of nonsense, and the only argument which is attempted is plainly fallacious and ill-considered. It is, of course, possible to formulate an argument using the compartmentalised approach, but you will, I suspect, find it very difficult to do it successfully within the various sections, because the structure itself inhibits argument. There is a very strong tendency to concentrate on putting facts or mere assertions into each compartment which militates against constructing an overall argument.

(c)   It is very difficult, particularly if you are just beginning, to know what to include in, and what to exclude from, each compartment. If no logical argument dictates what is to be included and excluded, there are no criteria by which to judge; experience, intuition or inspiration may be of help, but experience is not a reason, intuition is sometimes off colour and inspiration can be fitful.

The main difference between the two methods of construction, that in the form of an argument and that in the form of compartments, is one of presentation. The best method of presentation is to frame an argument based on sentencing principles and to arrange all your material relevant to your argument (relevance is all imporant), under topics or, if you will, compartments. The cardinal point in such a presentation is to make the facts subordinate to the argument and designed to illustrate and enliven it. This is in contrast to the compartmentalised approach in which facts are frequently asserted without argument and are confined within their compartments.

Illustrations are more vivid than precept and so it might be useful to consider how you might prepare a mitigation in a more complex case.

Suppose a case of robbery. The Prosecution allege that D took part in a Bank robbery, in which the robbers were armed with guns. They stole £150,000. A cashier was held at gunpoint while another robber emptied the safe. The robbers then escaped in a stolen car. D was arrested shortly after the robbery. He immediately made admission as to his part, saying that he was the driver. The police knew that to be true because his fingerprints were found on the steering wheel. D was prepared to help identify the other robbers and has given evidence against them in their trial. The defence instructions contain the following information.

D is 43 years old. In his teens he was convicted of theft (shoplifting), and after that three separate offences of dwelling-house burglary. He was put on probation for the first offence, but for the burglaries and breach of probation he received concurrent terms of Borstal training. At Borstal he qualified as an electrician. When released he got a job as an electrician which he held for about three years. Then he moved to a larger company where he was employed until two months before the offence took place. He was made redundant when the company was taken over by new management. Within about three weeks of his losing his job his wife left him and took their two children with her: two boys, Robert aged 14 and Darren aged 10.

On the day when the robbery occurred he went down to his local pub, and was having a drink by himself when a man came in. They struck up a conversation and he soon realised that he had met the man before, when they were in Borstal together. This man told him that he was a professional burglar. He said that he never did houses, only offices, shops and warehouses. He said that it so happened he had a job lined up that afternoon, and that he and his mates needed a driver to drive the car they had nicked for the job. D was asked if he wanted to come along as driver, and was told that he would get a 'couple of drinks' out of it. D says that he thought he was going to take part in a 'warehouse job', and had no idea that they intended to do an armed robbery of a bank. He emphasised in his instructions that he had no idea that they had guns till he got into the car and had a gun held to his own head. There were five other men in the car, a Mercedes, and he was told to drive to the small branch bank in a nearby town.

When they got to the bank, he was told to park nearby, and all five men got out. They were away about seven minutes and then came running back to the car. He says that three of the five men had sawn-off shot guns. He was told to drive into the countryside and they told him the route to take. As soon as they got outside town to a deserted spot he was told to get out of the car at gunpoint. He was given £150 and was told that if he 'grassed them up' he would be knee-capped, and was told that they knew where his children were. He says the car was then driven off and he did not see them again till they appeared in court.

You would be provided with this information in the form of the prosecution papers, instructions from the defence solicitors, and a statement from the defendant himself.

As you read these facts you will have noticed a number of possible mitigating factors as well as a number of vulnerable points in the defence

case. Once you have a good working knowledge of the facts the next step
is to analyse the sentencing principles which may be applicable to these
facts.

Here in note form is a summary of the law which you would have to
bear in mind in preparation. If I were actually preparing a case I would
make a similar summary and write in the margin the name of the authority
for each proposition. As the law as such is not within the scope of this book
I shall not litter the page with authorities, but they could be easily collated.

(1)   The tariff sentence for armed robbery of banks is 15 years. An
analysis of sentencing principles shows that the reason why this type of
offence attracts such heavy sentences are:

   (a)   because such offences require careful planning and usually
involve an organisation of professional criminals;

   (b)   because the fruits of the crime are likely to be very large, and

   (c)   because the firearms may be used to commit the crime or to
facilitate escape.
This last is the gravest aggravating factor.

You will see that if D's account is credible he can be dissociated from
these three aggravating features in large measure. His sentence therefore,
should, as a matter of principle, be very much lower than the normal 15
years.

(2)   A sentence may be discounted to some extent, where an offender,
though not of previously good character, has not exhausted credit for
good behaviour.

(3)   The judge is entitled to take into account the fact that the offence
was the result of emotional distress.

(4)   Likewise if the offence was committed as a result of serious
financial difficulties for which the offender was not wholly responsible.

(5)   The judge may have regard to the fact that the defendant will
have to serve part or all of his sentence in solitary confinement in order
to protect him from other prisoners.

(6)   The judge may also take account of the fact that the defendant
has given information to the police in order to bring other offenders to
book. Supergrasses often obtain substantial reductions in their sentences.

(7)   A plea of guilty almost always entitles the defendant to a discount
in sentence.

These seven general principles may have, in more or less degree, an
application to the plea that we are preparing. You should be looking for

any facts which could support an argument on one or other of these principles to reduce the sentence. Here is an analysis of the facts which might helpfully be used:

(1)   It is not alleged by the prosecution that D ever left the car during the robbery, so that his account that he did not play any part in what happened inside the bank is uncontradicted.

(2)   The fact that his fingerprints were found on the steering wheel is of considerable significance. If D had been involved in the planning of the robbery it is hardly likely that he would not have worn gloves to prevent his fingerprints being left in the car. Even if it was pointed out that it is surprising that he went to commit a burglary without gloves, the answer is that it shows that he went to the pub and then on to the car with the man who had recruited him, without knowing at the time he left home that he would be required to take part in the offence. It also suggests that he had no expectation of suddenly being ordered out of the car without any opportunity to wipe off his prints from the steering wheel where they were almost certain to be. In short, the fact that his prints were found, goes some way to confirm the account he has given of how he came to be involved and the part that he played. That account dissociates him to a large extent, if not entirely, from the three gravely aggravating features of the crime; planning, receipt of a large amount of money, and the carrying of firearms.

(3)   His plea of guilty.

(4)   His help to the police in naming the others, and his giving evidence for the Crown.

(5)   His account that he was given £150 in new notes should be carefully explored. Were the very notes recovered? If so, from where? Is there evidence of his having any other money in bank accounts or under the bed? If there is evidence which tends to establish that he only received £150 from the robbery, that evidence should be used to confirm D's account.

(6)   There are also some facts personal to the Defendant which might be used to invoke some of the other principles of sentencing which we have noted as possibly being relevant:

(a)   His staying out of trouble for so long after a bad start.

(b)   The emotional distress caused by the loss of his job and the desertion of his wife in quick succession.

In many cases there will be a pre-sentence report on the defendant. This will often contain useful information and a recommendation as to

sentencing options. You frequently can incorporate these recommendations into your argument with good effect; but a word of caution
is necessary. Be certain in your own mind that the suggestions made
by the probation officer are well-founded and realistic. There are
some officers who put forward wholly inappropriate recommendations.
The local judge will probably know which probation officers are sensible
and realistic, and will tend to ignore the reports of those whose views
he does not respect. Clearly you run the risk of weakening your argument
if you adopt a suggestion in a report which will carry no weight with
the judge.

So far we are doing well in getting together a number of strong points
in mitigation which can be woven into a formidable argument in favour
of a considerable reduction in the tariff sentence. But before we are ready
to arrange our argument in telling form we must consider the weak points
of D's account. To have spotted the weaknesses and to have thought
through a means of countering an attack is an essential part of good
preparation. If you are fully aware of the weaknesses of your case it will
help you to decide exactly what you want to say and equally important,
what you do not want to say. A good precept to observe, if you are afraid
of saying more than you ought, is to decide precisely what you are not
going to say and sticking to it.

The weak points in the defendant's acount which should be probed in
conference may be summarised in this way:

(a)   When he was made redundant what payment did he get? It should
have been considerable. What has he done with it? Was he really in
serious financial difficulties?

(b)   Had he really never seen the man who recruited him since
Borstal? How did they know that he had children and profess to know
where they were? What tempted him to take part in crime of any sort?

(c)   Were there really six men in the car? It is an odd fact because it
means that there was likely to be difficulty in jumping into the car in
making a getaway, which argues inept planning, and in addition six men
in a car might invite unwelcome attention.

Sufficient has been said to illustrate the kind of analysis which should
be made of the facts and the law. This method is no more than a technique
which will enable you to prepare an effective plea in mitigation, whatever
the case and whatever the court. Once you have acquired the technique
you can adapt it to suit your particular style.

The final task of preparation is to cast the plea into the form of a flowing whole. The aim will be to convince the judge by your argument. A note for a plea in this case might be on the following lines:

(1)   Sentence should be at the bottom end of the scale for this category of offence. Principles. 15 years the tarriff. Reasons. Planning. Fruits. Firearms. Defendant dissociated. His consistent account confirmed by fingerprints. £150 recovered in new notes.

(2)   Before commission of offence Borstal success. How did he become involved? Severe emotional distress: Job; Wife; Children;. Money; Financial settlement in divorce proceedings; redundancy gone on this.

(3)   Once agreed to participate could not extricate himself. Gunpoint. Courage in naming others and evidence for Crown.

(4)   Summary of above with a three or four year sentence in mind.

One advantage of the method of construction which I have recommended is that it will enable you to be confident that you will always have something realistic to say, which is likely to be of genuine assistance to the judge in his task of imposing sentence. A judge, after all, has a difficult duty to perform. It has often been said that it is easy to pass a severe sentence, and easy to pass a lenient one, but it is very difficult to get it right.

In a plea of mitigation you always start with one advantage. No judge wants to send a man to prison if, consistent with his duty to the public, he can avoid it. He will therefore be eager to hear and act on any argument which will enable him to pass the appropriate sentence, mitigated but not unnerved by mercy. If you always bear this in mind when making a plea, you will avoid the irrelevant, the sentimental and the absurd. It is difficult to over emphasise the importance of argument. Argument compels the judge to listen and to weigh your argument against any competing argument. If you are shrewd and have given the case due thought you will almost always be able to anticipate any argument which conflicts with yours, and you will do your best to undermine it.

It is useful if, during preparation, you have the particular judge in mind who is to hear the case. Elsewhere in this book I have discussed the importance of knowing the type of mind and the temperament of the judge you are addressing. It is always important to have this knowledge if you can get it, but it is nowhere more important than in a plea of mitigation. It is sometimes forgotten that judges like everyone else, have sympathies to which you can appeal and anathemas of which you should beware.

I think it was Lord Macmillan who said words to the effect that it is easy to be impartial between people, but it is much more difficult to be impartial between ideas. This is because, unless you are a 'don't know', knowing nothing, believing in nothing and standing for nothing, you acquire, as you go through life, strong convictions based on the values by which you live; and it is difficult to prevent yourself from being a prisoner of your own convictions.

If you are skilful in advocacy you will be able, sometimes, to influence a judge to come your way by a subtle appeal to his known convictions without his realising. But this is advocacy of the rarest kind, and is not to be confused with flattery or sycophancy. It depends upon a profound knowledge of the way in which the particular judge thinks and the values to which he refers in decision making, as well as an ability to say what you mean at more than one level of understanding.

Always try to be fresh and interesting. Judges listening to the same clichés, day in and day out, are easily captivated by the advocate who talks good sense, gives him an argument to found his sentence on, and who speaks pleasing English.

It is worth emphasising the importance of the use of appropriate language in a plea of mitigation because you as the advocate have it in your power to create the mood and feeling in court to a higher degree than usual. Perhaps this is because there is often a natural sympathy for an accused, whatever he has done, when he stands to be sentenced; and a corresponding eagerness to hear what can be said on his behalf. But whatever the reason, you should give special thought to the words in which you are going to express the key points of your mitigation, with an eye to the mood which you want to create. For example, you should not use slang expressions which reek of the underworld unless you wish to give a flavour of actuality to what you are saying, as for instance where you want to impress on the court that the defendant was acting under duress and you want to quote exactly the argot in which the threats to the defendant were expressed.

There is one word more to say about mitigation. Should you call a witness as to character? If so, when should you call him?

It often happens that a really good witness can do more for the defendant than all your eloquence and argument. If you are fortunate enough to have such a witness available you must call him. But never call a character witness without first seeing for yourself whether he is likely to be useful and reliable. One of the most important reasons for arriving early at court if you have a plea to do, is to give yourself the opportunity of speaking to any character witness who is available to give evidence. Such an interview will enable you to find out exactly what the witness will say, and perhaps more important, how he will say it. You will be able to assess whether the evidence supports the argument you intend to advance and to make your own assessment of the impression that the witness is likely to make on the court.

You should use your practical judgment as to when the witness should be called. A witness may be called at any time during the mitigation: it is up to you to decide. As a rule of thumb I would say that the best time to call the witness is at the outset of the defence case, before you have started on your plea. The reason for this advice is that you can often found your argument on the evidence of an impressive character witness. And on the other hand, if the witness does not come up to proof, and that quite frequently happens, you have a chance to recover the situation which you may not have if you call the witness at the end. I have seen more than once an excellent argument ruined by witnesses called at the end of mitigation who did not say anything like what they were expected to say.

Five

Examination in Chief

> *The Greeks had a recognised name for this ruse of*
> *saying much less than you mean, in the hope that your*
> *hearer's mind will make good even more than the large*
> *percentage of discount which you have deducted from*
> *the truth — cunning fellow, casting your bread on the*
> *waters, under the form of a kind of rebate, in sure and*
> *certain hope that it will return to you buttered. (C. E.*
> *Montague,* loc. cit., *47)*

The purpose of examination in chief is to lay before the tribunal all that
the witness knows which is relevant and material. Defining the purpose
in this way is intended to emphasise that the advocate should from first
to last be in control of the witness. When it is appreciated that the
advocate is not permitted to lead the witness on any material issue, that
is to say, he must not put words into the witness' mouth, the skill
necessary to accomplish his purpose is apparent. This chapter is an
attempt to show the technique by examples.

You must acquire a command of the rules of evidence which
particularly apply to questioning; only then will you be sure that the
questions you want to put will be unobjectionable, and equally important,
that you will not by your questions let in cross-examination which would
otherwise be inadmissible. You must, for example, have clear in your
mind the distinction between hearsay evidence, which is the statement of
a person other than the witness which, if admitted in evidence, is

designed to show the truth of the contents of that statement; and non-hearsay, which is the statement of a person other than the witness which when adduced in evidence shows simply that the statement was made and is not intended to show that the contents of the statement was true. The purpose of adducing non-hearsay evidence is usually to show the state of mind of the witness who is giving evidence. If the issue is whether the plaintiff bought a wig from Ede & Ravenscroft, the evidence of the plaintiff's brother that the manager of the shop told him that the plaintiff had bought a wig there last week is hearsay and inadmissible. If the Defendant to a criminal charge raises the defence of duress, and gives evidence that the reason he committed the alleged offence was because he had been threatened with death by bandits if he did not commit the crime, he is entitled to say what the bandits said to him. (See the leading authority of *Subramaniam* v *Public Prosecutor* [1956] 1 WLR 965.) Another example of an exclusionary rule is that normally a witness is not permitted to adduce evidence of a previous consistent statement. A defendant may not state in evidence that when he was charged, he went to his solicitor and made a written statement denying the allegation (see *R* v *Kurchid* (1984) Cr LR 288). If, on the other hand prosecution counsel were to put to the defendant that he had just, in the witness box, invented the explanation which he had advanced, the witness in re-examination could properly be asked to give in evidence the contents of the statement he made to his solicitor, immediately after charge, to show that the account given by him in the witness box was not a recent fabrication (*R* v *Oyesiku* (1972) 56 Cr App R 240).

An example of the danger of asking questions which would expose the witness to otherwise inadmissible cross-examination, is where a man with previous convictions is asked questions which tend to show that he is of good character. These examples are sufficient to illustrate the necessity of being completely familiar with the ambit of the rules of evidence which govern questioning.

The method of framing questions is a surprisingly difficult art to acquire. You will only gain a facility for it with constant practice, but it may be helpful to state a few rules upon which the technique of framing questions is based. Questions should be as short as possible; there should be no preamble to the question; do not 'suggest that' (see *R* v *Baldwin* (1925) 18 Cr App R 175). All questions should be single. Double questions are difficult to answer and are usually confusing both to the witness and to the court. Good questioning is dependant on clarity of thought. You must have a distinct idea of exactly what you intend to elicit by your question; this will enable you to frame precise questions. Here is an example taken from the *Archer-Shee* (*Celebrated Trials*, Ed. Ewen Montagu, 1974) case:

Q   What time was it you got leave to go, before or after lunch?
A   After lunch. Immediately after medical inspection.
Q   Who did you get leave from?
A   The cadet Gunner.
Q   What was the postal order you wanted to cash?
A   A ten shilling one.
Q   What order did you want to buy for yourself?
A   A two and sixpenny one.
Q   What was the name of the friend for whom you were going to buy another order?
A   Burton.
Q   How much was the order that he asked you to get for him?
A   Twelve shillings and three pence.
Q   You do not remember what amount he gave you?
A   No.

Notes.

(1)   Only the last question is a leading one (the leading elements in question one and five had been earlier established), yet the witness is under very close control. This control is achieved by the precision of the questions, which makes it difficult for the witness to elaborate even if he wanted to do so.

(2)   The order of the questions makes them easy for the witness to follow.

(3)   The reason for asking the last question in a leading form is evidently to prevent the witness from guessing. (The witness was aged 16.) The examiner doubtless had in mind that the witness was likely to be nervous which was an additional reason for keeping him on a tight rein.

In contrast to this example, suppose an inexperienced advocate dealing with the same points:

Q   Now James, just relax, you needn't be nervous, what we want to know, and you must be as accurate as possible, because this may be an important point in the case, is what time did you get leave to go and who did you get leave from?

Q Now you have already said that you wanted to cash a postal order, if you can remember exactly how much it was for, please tell us.

Q Are you sure?

Q You were going to buy a postal order for yourself you told us, if you remember, now can you remember, after all this time, how much you were going to buy it for, I mean how much was the postal order to be for?

Q Now, prior to your going to get the postal orders or to cash or buy them, you told us that a friend of yours, I think you said he was a friend, asked you to buy one for him. Now do you remember the name of this friend or have you forgotten after all this long time that has elapsed?

Q Now this postal order that you wanted him to get, or rather that he wanted you to get, how much was it for, do you remember that, just say if you can't remember.

Q Again don't hesitate to say if you can't remember, but can you say how much he gave you?

Notes.

(1)   These verbose questions are only slightly exaggerated for the purpose of illustration, but you will often hear this type of questioning in court. The first question has the admirable objective of putting the witness at ease, but that purpose is contradicted by the way in which the remainder of the question is phrased. The witness may be unnerved by being told what weight might be attributed to the answer on what he may think an unimportant point, and instead of giving the answer which springs to mind he may hedge from caution. In any event he will probably be confused by the double question.

(2)   The second question has the good intention of preparing the way for an unhelpful answer, as it provides the excuse of a natural lapse of memory. This is a matter of practical judgment: is the witness likely to falter? If so what is the most effective way of presenting the weakness in the evidence? We have seen how skilfully the examiner in the good examination solved the problem. He led the witness (see the last question).

(3)   The question 'are you sure?' is self-defeating. If the answer given was not the answer wanted, it will merely emphasise the error. If the answer was the one sought the question raises a doubt about it in the mind of the witness and of the tribunal. Something more will be said about this question, so frequently asked in examination in chief or in cross-

examination, but you would be well advised to expunge it from your vocabulary of questioning altogether.

(4)   The next question is merely confusing, because it is confused; but see also the impression which these questions are creating. It is one of a muddle, and it is beginning to appear that the examiner has no confidence at all in the ability of the witness to remember anything.

(5)   The next question is so poorly constructed that its point becomes lost in the verbiage. You should try to avoid using the word prior when you mean before because it is a word which some witnesses do not readily understand; it is a deviation from the rule of using plain words, if possible, in questioning.

(6)   The last two questions carry on the confusion. When the question is put the wrong way round it is simply because the examiner is not thinking clearly, and very likely his lack of preparation is also at fault.

Preparation for examination in chief begins with an appraisal of the contribution which the witness to be examined makes to the proof of the case or rebuttal of the other side. The first question may be whether it is necessary to call the witness at all. Sometimes the decision is a difficult one because while the witness may seem to make a useful contribution, it may be suspected that he will not come up to proof, or it may be that there is an aspect of his evidence which will be vulnerable to cross-examination. Only in rare circumstances will the advocate have an opportunity of seeing the witness and making a face-to-face assessment of him. It is of course permissible to see a party to proceedings in conference, to see experts, and to see witnesses who will give evidence only as to character. Because of these restrictions, when preparing the examination of a witness whom you may not interview, you will be dependant on the solicitor, or the person who prepared the proof of evidence. You may also be able to form an accurate impression of the evidence to be given from the way in which it is set out in the proof. It is quite surprising that frequently the character, attitude or bias of a witness becomes apparent on a careful reading of the proof even though it has been edited by the taker of the statement (not of course improperly, but to tidy it up). Proofs therefore should be read very carefully with a view to appraising the witness, and also, to enable you to become familiar with the way in which the witness expresses himself. This you will often find useful when examining the witness. Perhaps the witness forgets what he was going to say, or leaves out something contained in the proof which you need to elicit. If you have noted the order in which he dealt with the point in the proof and the vocabulary in which he expressed himself it may well be possible to take him over the ground again in the same order, and incorporate a key word used in the proof which will serve to remind the witness of the point. If in the example from the *Archer-Shee* case, the witness had forgotten or omitted the time when he got leave to go to the post office, the examiner might have asked him whether there was a medical inspection that day, then establish the time of the inspection, and then ask whether he obtained leave before or after it, and if necessary how soon after it.

If the proof of the witness has been well taken and it is in chronological order, or some other satisfactory order, it will suffice if you use it as it stands. If the proof is very long and contains some irrelevant matter, or dodges about from point to point and back again, you should make an extract for your own use. This should contain all the relevant material, set out in the order in which you plan to adduce it from the witness. Your aim should be to carry in your head all the points to be dealt with by the witness. If that is a counsel of perfection, the next best thing is to have as an aid to memory all the relevant material set out in order in trigger notes. The reason for this advice is that you should aim to watch the witness all the time when you are examining. Facial expression and gestures are often a good guide to the examiner as to the way in which he should handle the witness, and besides that, the confidence of the witness is likely to be increased if the advocate is speaking to him as though in conversation with him. A really good examination should leave the tribunal with the impression that the witness has given his own account of the matters in issue without prompting. In this conversation with the witness you should make sure that you speak distinctly and try to get the witness to do the same.

The manner in which you ask your questions is bound to influence the way in which they are answered. It should be an invariable rule that you treat witnesses with courtesy and patience. You should have your own temper under perfect control, and you should not betray your feelings if you get a disappointing answer. You sometimes see the inexperienced advocate throw his eyes to the ceiling on receiving a half-witted answer or looking downcast at one that seems to damage his case. If you do get such answers, and you will, just go on in the same easy manner as though nothing untoward had happened.

With his accustomed sureness of touch, Dickens in *Pickwick Papers* depicted in Sam Weller the epitome of the unhelpful witness.

Q Now Mr Weller [said Sergeant Buzfuz].

A Now Sir, replied Sam.

Q I believe you are in the service of Mr Pickwick the defendant in this case. Speak up if you please Mr Weller.

A I mean to speak up sir. I am in the service of that 'ere gen'l'man and a wery good service it is.

Q Little to do and plenty to get I suppose.

A Oh, quite enough to get sir, as the soldier said ven they ordered him three hundred and fifty lashes.

Q Do you recollect anything particular happening on the morning when you were first engaged by the defendant; eh Mr Weller?

A Yes I do sir.

Q Have the goodness to tell the jury what it was.

A I had a reg'lar new fit out of clothes that mornin' gen'l'man of the jury ... and that was a wery partickler and uncommon circumstance with me in those days.

Q Do you mean to tell me Mr Weller ... do you mean to tell me that you saw nothing of this fainting on the part of the plaintiff in the arms of the defendant which you have heard described by the witness?

A Certainly not; I was in the passage till they called me up, and then the old lady was not there.

Q Now attend Mr Weller [said Sergeant Buzfuz, dipping a large pen into the ink stand before him, for the purpose of frightening Sam with a show of taking down his answer], you were in the passage, and yet saw nothing of what was going forward. Have you a pair of eyes Mr Weller?

A Yes, I have a pair of eyes, and that's just it. If they was a pair o' patent double million magnifyin' gas microscopes of hextra power, p'raps I might be able to see through a flight o' stairs and a deal door; but bein' only eyes, you see, my wision's limited.

Q Now Mr Weller, I'll ask you a question on another point, if you please.

A If you please sir.

Q Do you remember going up to Mrs Bardell's house, one night in November last?

A Oh, yes, very well.

Q Oh, you do remember that Mr Weller, ... I thought we should get at something at last.

A I rayther thought that too sir.

Q Well, I suppose you went up to have a little talk about this trial — eh
    Mr Weller? [said Sergeant Buzfuz, looking knowingly at the jury].

A I went up to pay the rent; but we did get a talkin' about the trial.

Q Oh you did get a talking about the trial.... Now what passed about
    the trial; will you have the goodness to tell us Mr Weller.

A Vith all the pleasure in life sir ... arter a few unimportant
    obserwations from the two wirtuous females as has been examined
    here today, the ladies get into a wery great state o' admiration at the
    honourable conduct of Mr Dodson and Fogg — them two gen'l'man
    as is settin' near you now.

Q The attorney's for the plaintiff.... Well, they spoke in high praise of
    the honourable conduct of Messrs Dodson and Fogg, the attorneys
    for the plaintiff did they?

A Yes, ... they said what a wery generous thing it was o' them to have
    taken up the case on spec. and to charge nothing at all for costs, unless
    they got 'em out of Mr Pickwick.

    [Sergeant Buzfuz] It's perfectly useless, my Lord, attempting to get
    at any evidence through the impenetrable stupidity of this witness. I
    will not trouble the Court by asking him any more questions. Stand
    down sir.

    [Weller] Would any other gen'l'man like to ask me any questions?

    [Sergeant Snubbin, laughing] Not I, Mr Weller, thank you.

For our purposes it is worth dwelling on the numerous mistakes which
Sergeant Buzfuz made in this examination. Dickens' parody is uncom-
fortably close to reality, and the mistakes made frequently occur in court
nowadays.

Notes.

    (1) Mr Weller should never have been called. He may well have been
a witness for the defence in which case he could have been cross-
examined. (He would undoubtedly have outwitted the Sergeant in that
event too.)

    (2) It is apparent that the examiner has little or no idea what Weller
is going to say. It is a fundamental rule of examination never to call a
witness without knowing what he is likely to say. Even if a surprise
witness turns up during the course of a case, seek an adjournment if
necessary, for a proof to be taken before calling him.

    (3) Buzfuz was hoping to establish by Weller's evidence that
Pickwick was discovered holding the plaintiff in his arms, and 'soothing

her agitation by his caresses and endearments'. That is how he opened it.
He had already obtained this evidence from Mr Winkle and Mrs Cluppins
and therefore calling Weller was quite pointless. The way in which he
should have sought this evidence from Weller, had it been necessary to
call him, might have been somewhat on these lines.

Q   Were you first employed by Mr Pickwick in July last year?
Q   On the first day of your employment were you at Mrs Bardell's
     house?
Q   Did you see Mr Pickwick there?
Q   At any time during the morning did you see him with Mrs Bardell?
Q   In which room of the house?
Q   At about what time was that?
Q   Was anyone else in the room at that time?
Q   Who?
Q   Was Mrs Bardell well or unwell during the time you were in the room?
Q   How did her illness show itself?
Q   When she was taken ill, what did Mr Pickwick do?
Q   What did he say?
Q   When he said that, how was he speaking, gently or roughly?

It may, of course, be that Weller did not see them together at any time. If
that was his answer, then Buzfuz should have stopped there. At least the
witness would have done him no harm. You will see from these suggested
questions that once the witness' mind had been brought to the occasion
by permissible leading questions, precise questions are asked which
make it very difficult, even for such a deliberately awkward witness, to
slip away from the point of the question. The examiner should, in any
case, have observed from an incident that occurred before the passage
quoted that Weller, while astute enough to evade any question that he did
not wish to answer, would avoid telling a direct lie. Weller's father had
made a disturbance in court; the judge asked him if he could see him here
now: ''No, I don't my Lord,' replied Sam, staring right up into the lantern
of the roof of the Court.'

    (4)   By contrasting the proposed questions with those actually asked
it is easy to see how Buzfuz went wrong from the outset. To begin with,
his manner is overbearing and likely to provoke hostility in a witness of
much less spirit than Weller. Next his attempt at a quip at both Pickwick's
and Weller's expense was wholly out of place. It could not serve his
purpose in eliciting what he wanted from the witness, but he could not
resist the opportunity to try to be funny.

The question 'do you remember anything particular happening . . .' is the type of open question which is asked in court every day. It is too loose a question to be satisfactory: apart from the deliberately obstructive witness like Sam, there are many who would genuinely be baffled by the question. Their reaction to it is that several particular things happened, and they do not know which one to mention. You will see in the suggested questions how the difficulty is overcome. The witness is directed to the time of year and the day in question by leading. It is unobjectionable because there is no issue as to when Weller began his employment. Having got him to the day, the witness, again by proper leading, is taken to the incident and if he is at all inclined to cooperate he will give the evidence required without further leading. It is evident that some ingenuity is usually needed to be sure of bringing the mind of the witness to the relevant point, and you should think out the way in which you will do it with each witness when the date of the incident is in issue. Look for some point in the evidence that the witness is to give that is likely to be a fixed point in his mind. An effective fall back is to ask the witness whether he has come to court to give evidence about a particular incident which he witnessed.

(5)   In his exasperation Buzfuz gives up all pretence of not leading, and plunges into the matter of the fainting by a grossly leading question; but even that fails and was likely to fail because of the hostile way in which he phrased the question. The fundamental reason for avoiding leading questions on matters in issue is that the answer to such a question is made so much weaker because the answer has been prompted.

(6)   The theatrical gesture should be avoided. Even in the days of Marshall Hall, the dramatic phrase or gesture was apparently acceptable; but not now. In the 1960s it almost seemed as though it was necessary to be inarticulate to be thought sincere. Perhaps there has been a move away from that extreme position, but we are none the less living in a time which George Steiner has called the 'age of embarrassment'. So dipping a large pen into the inkstand with the purpose of frightening Sam was the kind of ham acting which should play no part in modern advocacy.

(7)   After receiving Sam's devastating reply to 'Have you a pair of eyes Mr Weller?' Buzfuz in his confusion embarks on a line of questioning which is evidently unprepared. All he knows is that there was a visit to Mrs Bardell's and he hopes to obtain some information from the witness which will make it appear that Pickwick, through his servant, was trying to influence the course of the trial. Again he blunders in with an open-ended question which allows the witness to say what he likes,

and Sam neatly leads him on to think he is at last saying something helpful. Buzfuz falls for the ploy, instead of stopping his examination on a relatively favourable point. In questioning of any sort you should abide by the maxim that better is the enemy of good. When you have got what you want, stop.

(8)   The attempt at the end to extricate himself from the damaging answers that Sam has given him is, needless to say, quite unacceptable. In any event it is only too plain that the contempt which he expressed for Weller's mental abilities should have been reserved for his own.

Mention has already been made of the use and avoidance of leading questions in examination in chief; and the essential point is that you may not lead on matters in issue, but you may, and indeed should lead on preliminary matters. As has also been observed, the skilful use of leading questions can be of very great value in keeping a witness under firm control. A further illustration of the way in which this should be done may be useful.

The illustration is from the *Archer-Shee* case upon which Terance Rattigan's well known play 'The Winslow Boy' was based. The main point at issue was whether George Archer-Shee, who was a naval cadet at Osborne Royal Naval College, had stolen, forged and cashed, a postal order for 5 shillings. He was dismissed from the College, without a fair hearing. His family protested. They struggled for three years to obtain a hearing. Sir Edward Carson represented the boy. Sir Rufus Isaacs, the Crown. In brief the facts were that cadets at Osborne had to bank their money with the appropriate officer. George had £2. 3s. banked, and over £4 in the post office which he could have drawn out with authorisation. On the day in question he wanted to buy an engine for 15s. 6d. He asked the officer for permission to draw 16s.; permission was granted. On Wednesday 7 October 1908, Cadet Terence Back, a member of George's term, received a 5s. postal order. He could not remember whether any other cadet knew of his receipt of the order. Certainly George denied that he knew of it until he was told by Back that it was lost. Back put the order in a writing-case in his locker in the Drake reading room; it was not locked. After medical inspection, George got his 16s. from the paymaster. He took the money to his locker in the reading room. He was not strictly allowed to go to the reading room at that time, and there was no apparent reason for him to do so. He put the money into his locker and then went to his dormitory to change his uniform. He then went outside where he spoke to Cadet Scholes and asked him to go with him to the post office. Scholes refused. George then went to the reading room and collected his money. He said in evidence, that on his return from the reading room to the flagstaff he again met Scholes, again invited him to accompany him to the post office and was again refused. Scholes denied this at first in his evidence but eventually conceded that it was possible that it happened. George then went to the post office. The time at which he went was an important issue. He said at first that it was between 3.00 p.m. and 4.00 p.m., but said that was a slip which he corrected almost immediately, and the time was in fact 2.30 p.m. It is perhaps significant that it was a breach of rules to go into the reading room between 2-3 p.m. It follows from his correction of the time that George went into the reading room twice against the rules.

One other cadet, James Arbuthnot, got leave to go to the post office that afternoon. He went at about 2.30 p.m. He cashed a postal order for 10*s*. bought one for himself for 2*s*. 6*d*. and another for a friend for 12*s*. 6*d*. He then returned to the college.

The crucial evidence in the case was that of the post mistress Miss Tucker. On the day following the commission of the offence she signed a statement to the effect that only two cadets came to do business with postal orders on the afternoon of Wednesday, 7 October 1908. The first one cashed a postal order for 10*s*. and bought one for 12*s*. 3*d*. and another for 2*s*. 6*d*. The second one bought a postal order for 15*s*. 6*d*. and cashed one for 5*s*. 'I swear that the cadet who bought the postal order for 15*s*. 6*d*. also cashed one for 5*s*. which was made payable to, and was signed, Terence Back'. Before she made that statement she had attended the college, and was given a chance to see, and hear speaking, George, Arbuthnot and some other cadets who were thought to be aware of the existence of the postal order. She was unable to identify either George or Arbuthnot. She said that all the cadets looked alike when they just came into the post office in uniform.

George said that he bought his postal order and a penny stamp for the letter; he paid for them with the 16*s*. and had a discussion with Miss Tucker about the amount of his change, telling her that he was unfamiliar with the cost of a postal order. He then returned to college. From first to last he denied that he had cashed the 5*s*. postal order. When he got back to college he went to the reading room to write off for his engine and was there told by Cadet Back of the theft of the postal order. He always maintained that was the first time he had heard of its existence.

The main issues in the case can be collected from this account. They were:

(a)   Did George know of the existence of Back's postal order before he went to the post office in the afternoon?

(b)   If he stole it, why did he draw attention to himself by getting leave to go to the post office?

(c)   Why did he put the 16s. in the locker room? There was no real reason for him to do so, and therefore was consistent with the Crown case that his only reason for doing so was to enable him to take Back's postal order; and if challenged in going or coming away, he would have an excuse at the ready for being there.

(d)   Did he ask Scholes for a second time to accompany him to the post office? If so it is hardly likely that he stole the postal order, because it would have meant that Scholes might possibly go with him to the post office, when he had the stolen postal order in his possession. Alternatively, did he make up the account of speaking to Scholes a second time in order to provide himself with the argument just stated?

(e)   Was there room for error in Miss Tucker's evidence?

(f)   Had there been any other instances of pilfering in the college at about that time?

This brief analysis of the main issues is an example of the way in which you should prepare your case. Such an analysis enables you to be aware, throughout the conduct of the case, of what really matters.

We are now in a position to look in detail at the way in which Sir Edward Carson examined George Archer-Shee.

Q   We know George [he was aged 16] that you were educated at Stonyhurst?

A   Yes.

Q   We know that you went to Osborne in January 1908?

A   Yes.

Q   And you had also passed the necessary education examination?

A   Yes.

Q   In the same term as yourself was there a boy named Terence H. Back?

A   Yes.

Q   [Mr Justice Phillimore] The boys keep together. What is called the 'term' means that the boys in one term keep together?

A   Yes, that is so.

Q   And each term keeps to itself?

A   Yes, each term keeps to itself.

Q   [Sir Edward Carson] How many boys would there be in a term?

A   From 60 to 70.

Q   And they I suppose would occupy two dormitories?

A   Yes.

Q   Had each dormitory its own reading rooms?

A   Yes.

Q   Are the dormitories and the reading rooms on the same floor?

A   Yes.

Q   The whole accommodation for the boys, I think, is on one floor?

A   Yes it is.

Q   You have a long dormitory and reading rooms on the opposite side of the passage?

A   Yes.

Q   And you can come in and out off the playground into the passage that leads to the dormitory and the reading rooms?

A   Yes.

Q   Were the boys put into the dormitories alphabetically?

A   Yes.

Q   [Mr Justice Phillimore] Did you pass as Shee or Archer-Shee?

A   Archer-Shee, My Lord.

Q   [Sir Edward Carson] As a matter of fact — I do not know how long it continued — were you in the dormitory next to Back?

A   Yes.

Q   Did you continue down to the end of the time you were there?

A   Yes, right up to the end.

Q   In the reading room had each of the cadets lockers?

A   Yes.

Q   And are they allotted alphabetically?

A   Yes, as near as they can, in the same way as the dormitories.

Q   In the same way was your locker next to Back's?

A   Yes.

Q   Was that just inside the door or where?

A   Just inside the door to the left.

Q   In your dormitory do you have a chest?

A   Yes.

Q   Is that a large box?

A   Yes, and it is placed at the end of each cadet's bed.

Q   Is that a sea chest such as they take to sea with them?

A   It is called a sea chest.

Q   It is a large chest that you put clothes in, and I dare say many other things?

A   Yes.
Q   In that chest is there also a till?
A   Yes.
Q   Is the till fastened by a hasp, and has it got a lock of its own?
A   It has a lock of its own.
Q   In addition to the sea chest having a lock?
A   Yes.
Q   A separate lock?Yes.
Q   Not the same key?
A   No.
Q   Are the lockers in the reading room locked?
A   No they are not.
Q   Have they no locks?
A   No.
Q   We know that you went back to the college on the 18th of September?
A   Yes, as far as I can remember, I think that was the date.
Q   Did you, when you went back to the college have money with you?
A   Yes.
Q   How much?
A   As far as I can remember, I think it was about £2. 10*s*.
Q   It must have been the 18th. You went back, I think, because I see on
      the 19th of September 1908, you deposited £2. 17*s*.?
A   Yes.
Q   On the 23rd of September I see you drew out 4*s*., leaving £2. 13*s*. and
      on the 30th September you drew out 10*s*.?
A   I do not remember these withdrawals.
Q   You may take it from me. That left you with £2. 3*s*. which you
      had on the morning of the 7th of October. In addition to that you
      had, I think, on deposit in the Post Office Savings Bank, a sum of
      money?
A   Yes.
Q   Is this your book? [Handed to the witness.]
Q   [Mr Justice Phillimore] Is that of any importance? He could not get
      it out could he?
A   [Sir Edward Carson] Yes, my Lord, he could get it by applying to the
      post office. Your Lordship will find in the documents that it is
      admitted for the purpose of this action that Archer-Shee had at that
      time £4. 3*s*. 11*d*. in the Savings Bank.
Q   [Mr Justice Phillimore] His book shows £5. 7*s*. and there is 14*s*. or
      thereabouts, drawn out.

A [Sir Edward Carson] He had withdrawn 14*s*. and 10*s*. and consequently £4. 3*s*. 11*d*. remained.

Q Was Wednesday the day for drawing out money?

A Yes.

Q Will you just tell us when you wanted to get out money from the
paymaster, what you had to do?

A If you wanted more than two shillings, you had to get a chit signed
by the Lieutenant of your term stating what you wanted it for, and
then, after the medical inspection, fall in and take it to the paymaster
and hand it in. Then he would give you the amount, provided it was
signed by your Lieutenant.

Q Who was the Lieutenant of your term?

A Lieutenant Burrows.

We have now reached the point in the examination when Carson is about
to turn to the specific events of the day when the 5*s*. postal order was
stolen, forged and cashed. Let us therefore take stock of the way in which
he has examined so far.

Notes.

(1) It is plain that Carson has a complete command of the facts of the
case, down to the smallest detail. He is almost certainly examining from
his head, to be sure he will not have been delving into his brief in order
to see what question he should ask next!

(2) In dealing with the background to the case he has divided
the story into topics. He deals with each topic completely and in an
orderly fashion before passing to the next topic. That is an important
element in good examination, because it is much easier for the witness to
deal fully with the topic while his mind is playing on it, and from the
tribunal's point of view it is easy to follow and note. It is sometimes quite
exasperating for a judge trying to note the evidence if the advocate darts
to and fro, from point to point. A third reason is a psychological one; when
a topic is dealt with fully there is a feeling that it is convincing because it is
complete.

(3) You will have seen that Carson in this examination has led the
witness all the time, with the exception of a very few questions. We
should consider first why he has done so, and secondly whether it is a
good model to follow. His reasons for leading in this way seem to have
been these:

(a)   The topics which he has dealt with so far are not in issue.
(b)   He is determined to keep as tight a rein on the witness as possible.

George is a boy of 16, speaking about events which happened three years before and whom he knows will be cross-examined by Isaacs who will miss nothing. He therefore does not want the witness to elaborate his evidence beyond what is strictly necessary for fear of providing material for cross-examination. Carson knows the weaknesses in George's account, and he also knows that Isaacs has some material which he will certainly use. For example, that George had told Commander Cotton on 8 October that the reason he had written 'Terence H. Back' when asked by him to do so, was because he and Back had been practising one another's signatures in the reading room two or three days before. Carson had to make a practical decision whether to deal with this matter in chief. His decision not to deal with it was evidently because the point was strictly irrelevant because it was not suggested that the signature on the postal order was an attempt to make the post mistress believe that Back had signed it because there was not the slightest suggestion that she knew Back's signature.

An additional reason for leading seems to have been in order to give some confidence to the witness. As to whether leading in this way is a good model to follow, there can be no doubt that the kind of control exercised over the witness is in many cases highly desirable. A balance must, of course, be struck between allowing the witness to give his own account in his own words and keeping the witness to the point and preventing him from elaborating in such a way as to give away material for cross-examination. This is in every case a matter of practical judgment for the advocate. I would say that if you want to exercise the tightest control over a witness, then Carson's examination of George is a perfect example of how to do it; but I would add as a cautionary note that he went, as we shall see, too far with leading when he came to a critical point of the evidence and, I think, had it been any less powerful personality he would have been stopped and possibly reprimanded by the judge. That, of course, would have been most undesirable because it might materially have affected the view the jury took of George's evidence. As to leading on the matters which were not in issue, that is to say all the examination so far reviewed, there could be no objection save perhaps this. It is often a good policy for the examiner to give the witness his head on non-material matters to get him used to expressing himself from the witness box before coming to the points in issue on which it is not permissible to lead.

(4)   The questions asked are almost invariably short and pointed. Each topic is explored step by step. You will have spotted one double question. Even Homer nods.

(5)   The fact that George's locker was next to Back's tends to make the mind jump to the conclusion that it strengthens the case against George. In order to counter this unjustified conclusion Carson has very skilfully placed the fact in its context. The boys were in dormitories alphabetically. In the same way the lockers in the reading room were arranged alphabetically.

(6)   Carson used the post office book to refresh the memory of the witness. This is a very useful tactic with a witness whose memory is shaky. The rule of evidence is that a witness may refresh his memory from a contemporaneous document which he himself has made or had an opportunity of checking while the matters dealt with in the document were fresh in his mind. You should be familiar with the various authorities on this question so that you can make use of the rule (to its extremity) when examining a witness. Always note the date when the witness' statement was made. If it was made reasonably contemporaneously you will probably be able to persuade the judge to allow the witness to refer to it to refresh his memory (see for example *R* v *Richardson* [1971] 2 QB 484).

(7)   The way in which Carson dealt with the interventions of the judge shows that he not only knew his case in detail, but was also able to justify the relevance of his questions. An advocate should never state anything in court which he is not able to justify. That is sometimes a difficult maxim to follow, but if it is followed you will find it of great value. It will often prevent you from putting yourself in the wrong in the heat of the moment. Its restraining influence will make you think through propositions of fact and law which you might otherwise neglect.

The continuation of Carson's examination deals with topics concerning the day of the alleged offence and the circumstances of his expulsion from Osborne. It might be instructive to see in summary form the topics which Carson decided to deal with and the order in which he dealt with them. This summary may also serve as an example of the sort of note which you could use in conducting an examination. The advantage of having such a note to hand is that you can ensure that each topic is dealt with fully, in your chosen order, and that you leave nothing out.

(a)   The amount of money he wanted to obtain.
(b)   The time-table for the Wednesday, from breakfast to evening.

(c)   The time of the medical inspection (from 1.40 p.m.-2.00 p.m.).

(d)   What he did with the money once he had obtained it.

(e)   After putting the money in his locker, and getting changed, what he did then.

(f)   Meeting Scholes for the first time and what was said.

(g)   Fetching the money from the locker.

(h)   Second meeting with Scholes.

(i)   Obtaining leave to go to the post office.

(j)   The distance of the post office from college and whether it was out of bounds.

(k)   The lay out of the post office (important because it was George's case that the post mistress may have had her back turned as George left and someone else came in with the 5s. order).

(l)   What happened in the post office when he bought his order.

(m)   His denial of cashing any order.

(n)   His return to college and what he did. Reporting his return. His going immediately afterwards to the reading room.

(o)   His seeing and speaking to Back. Learning for the first time of the existence of the 5s. order.

(p)   Sending off his order and his uncertainty as to whether he should sign his name on it. (The person who had cashed the 5s. order had signed it.)

(q)   First interview with Commander Cotton next morning. His writing 'Terence H. Back' when asked by Cotton to write Back's name in full. And the explanation he gave at the time. (Note particularly that Carson did not explore the reason any further. He foresaw that Isaacs would deal with it in cross-examination because George was alleged to have said during the college investigation that he and Back had, a few days before, practised each other's signatures. George had no recollection of saying any such thing. Carson no doubt wanted to see what use Isaacs would make of the point knowing that he could re-examine if necessary.)

(r)   His second interview with Cotton that day, and what was said.

(s)   His interview with the Captain and his saying he went to the post office about 2.30 p.m. and that nothing was said about 3.30 p.m.

(t)   His dismissal from the college 12 days later and his denial of the charge from first to last.

Before leaving Carson's examination of George I shall focus attention on one or two of these topics to comment specifically on the method adopted by him. Let us look at point (f) — meeting Scholes for the first time and what was said:

Q   Did you see a cadet named Scholes there?
A   Yes, he was waiting for friends.
Q   Was he a friend of yours?
A   Yes.
Q   Did you say anything to Scholes?
A   I asked him to come with me to the post office.
Q   Did you say for what?
A   I told him I was going to get a postal order for 15s. 6d.
Q   Did you say for what purpose you wanted it? Do you remember?
A   I cannot remember.
Q   Did you then after that go to get your money?
A   Yes, I did.
Q   Did you go to your locker?
A   Yes.
Q   And you got your money and came out?
A   Yes.
Q   [The Solicitor General] He had better tell the story himself. This is important here.
Q   [Sir Edward Carson] Very well. Did you see Scholes again then?
A   Yes, he was in the same place.

Notes.

(1)   The question 'Was he a friend?' is important in the account which is being presented. The thinking behind it is to place the conversation in context. What would be a natural and likely request to a friend might seem odd if he were only an acquaintance. It is this kind of small touch which can affect the overall impression made by the witness.

(2)   The next two questions are non-leading but are phrased so as to get the answers which are wanted. The following question is again skilful. Carson almost certainly knows that George cannot remember whether he told Scholes the purpose for which he wanted the money. By introducing the doubt as to his memory in the question, makes the answer more credible. The impression being created is 'Here is a boy, when he does not remember, saying he does not remember'.

(3)   After Isaacs had intervened to try to prevent Carson leading, the next question asked is, in fact, leading. This question is strongly to be criticised. It exposed Carson to a stinging rebuke from the judge; or a protest from Isaacs. A rebuke or a protest would have had the effect of

underlining the impression in the minds of the jury that George was not being allowed to tell his own story. Carson must have had a strong reason for taking this risk. It was probably because he knew that Scholes himself denied that there was a second conversation, and he wanted to be certain that George did not flicker in his recollection of it. It was the kind of instant decision that the advocate is frequently called on to make, and one which is usually made instinctively according to the 'feel' of the moment.

Carson continued:

Q What happened then?
A I asked him again to come to the post office.
Q What did he say?
A He said he could not come because he was waiting for friends.
Q Can you recollect how Scholes was dressed?
A He had flannels on and a monkey jacket and a cap. I am not sure if he had a sweater.
Q What did you do then?
A When I had asked him the second time, I started off for the post office.
Q Before that did anything happen?
A Not to my recollection.
Q Did you see Paul?
A Yes.
Q Will you tell us what happened?
A I went to look for the petty officer. I looked to see who the petty officer of the day was, and I saw that it was chief petty officer Paul. Then I went to look for him and when I found him, I asked leave, and he gave it to me. He told me to report myself when I came back, and then I started off.
Q Do you remember or can you tell us, whether the time you asked for leave was before or after you asked Scholes the second time?
A I could not be certain of that.
Q [Mr Justice Phillimore] Paul told you to report yourself as soon as you came back?
A Yes.
Q Would that be to report to him?
A Yes.
Q [Sir Edward Carson] Can you remember whether it was before or after you asked Scholes for the first time, you got leave?
A It was after I asked him for the first time.

Notes.

(1)   Asking how Scholes was dressed at this point is a subtle, well thought out question. It should be observed that it was not asked at the time of dealing with the first meeting with Scholes. The reason for delaying the question was to add weight and colour to the recollection of the second meeting. By associating his recollection of how Scholes was dressed with the second meeting it helps to create the impression that there was indeed a second meeting.

(2)   It is interesting to see that as soon as Carson stopped leading, George had a lapse of memory. Carson immediately put it right by asking 'Did you see Paul?'. This was to some extent a leading question, but it was neatly done to avoid objection by simply referring to him as Paul. He did not refer to him as chief petty officer Paul, which would have been grossly leading and would have diminished the effect of the evidence. Simply mentioning the name Paul was sufficient to bring the mind of the witness to the point that he had omitted and his evidence was then adduced naturally and easily.

(3)   Carson is not deflected by the judge's intervention from establishing as far as he is able the time when George saw Paul. The effect of this evidence is again designed to add weight to the recollection that Scholes was seen on two occasions.

The next example is taken from an ordinary case such as is frequently heard in the Crown Court. The defendant who is examined (Mr Z) was charged with conspiracy to obtain property by deception. He was a metal dealer and a director of a large national company with many subsidiaries. His base was at A Metals, but he travelled round the country to other subsidiaries.

It was alleged that drivers at A Metals were working a weighbridge fraud when delivering to B Metals. The method used was to bribe the weighbridge men to issue tickets which showed that more metal had been delivered to B Metals than was true. Thus A Metals would be paid substantially more than they should have been by B Metals. Payment was always made by cheque. The case against the drivers was very strong, but Mr Z's defence was that they were working a fiddle on their own. They were, according to him, going out with a fully loaded lorry, selling some of the load as they went from A to B, and putting the proceeds into their own pockets. Then when they got to B they would bribe the weighbridge men to issue a ticket which showed the weight that had originally been on the lorry. The only evidence against Z was that when

interviewed by police, although denying the allegation, he had made
some equivocal remarks. The drivers and the manager (Q) at A Metals
were also charged in the conspiracy, and when interviewed by police,
said that Mr Z was the person who paid them to commit the offence and
to bribe the weighbridge men. The manager at trial denied that the
statement he had made was true, and said that he had made it because he
wanted to get out of the police station because of some pressing personal
problem which made it imperative to secure his release as soon as was
possible. By the time Mr Z gave evidence, Q had given his account in the
witness box. His defence was similar to that of Mr Z; he said that the
drivers were only trying to shift the seriousness of the offence from off
their own shoulders.

The first point to make is that it was highly questionable whether it was
necessary to call Mr Z at all. As will be seen from his answers, he was a
voluble man, confident in his ability to create a good impression with the
jury and thus very difficult for the examiner to keep under control. The
examiner chose to examine this witness in considerable detail about his
position in the company and the nature of his work. He evidently decided
that the best way of presenting him was to let him create a picture of a
good-natured, moderately intelligent, successful and innocent business
man.

Q I just want to ask you a little bit about your connection with Boyces.
    How long have you been connected with Boyces if I can use that
    rather general term?
A 31 years.
Q What were you before you went into Boyces?
A I was a barber, a hairdresser.
Q During the whole of the 31 years you have been working with metal
    have you?
A Yes.
Q When you went into it what sort of size company was it?
A Well, it was just a small company, with about six or eight employees
    at the time.
Q Was Mr Boyce the head of it?
A Yes.
Q As he is today?
A Yes.
Q Was it a limited company then, or just a firm? or don't you know?
A I'm not quite sure. I think it was a limited company.

Q Now your own position, you are a director of the parent company aren't you?

A I am, yes.

Q Are you the director of any of the subsidiary companies?

A Yes, quite a few. There were two working directors in the company; Mr Boyce and myself.

Q What was your connection with the A company?

A Well at the time when I went there it was one of these companies that never had a manager. We had Mr Q who ran the yard, and the place used to run itself. You didn't really need anyone there, but it was decided that as there was no overall manager, when I was in London I would base myself there, so if any problem came up they could come to me.

Q Were you a signatory of the cheques at A company?

A Well being a director of the main board, I was basically a signatory of the whole — you know I could go to any sort of company and sign a cheque there.

Q Concentrating for the moment on A company, how often were you called upon to write cheques, or didn't you sign cheques at A Company?

A Yes, I signed cheques there.

Q A lot of them?

A In the early days, when I first went there, when Mr Jones was alive, I never signed any. After he died, I used to be the only signatory, I think, and what used to happen was that the young cashier, she used to ask me to sign a dozen at a time, so that she always had signed cheques in the office. I thought that was a little bit dangerous, so we introduced a security officer, who also became a signatory.

Q Who drew up the cheques for signature?

A Normally the cashier.

Q If she did not draw them up, who did?

A She drew. She was the cashier, she made all the cash — she made up all the cash cheques, I think, or the security officer. She would tell him they need some cash, and he would write them out. The book keeper used to invariably write them out — about once a month he would get all the bills and he would pay them out, and he would write out a load of cheques with the various accounts; and occasionally — well invariably, if I was there, he would ask me if I would sign them.

Notes.

The witness has gradually been getting out of control and this last answer is more or less incomprehensible. The witness has already disclosed himself as a witness who will ramble on without any regard to precision. He has said contradictory things in the course of the same answer, and seems quite unaware of it. The tribunal is thus left with the impression that he is not a careful witness. In addition the evidence he has so far given is extremely boring. That sometimes cannot be helped, but in this instance it could have been avoided because this evidence is entirely unnecessary. You will have observed however, that the examiner has been asking short questions and yet the answers go rambling on. What has gone wrong? It is true that the witness is prone to talk without thinking, a most difficult type of witness. The trouble is that although the questions are short, they are not sufficiently pointed; in addition the examiner does not direct the witness to answer the question which has been asked. We have already seen how leading questions can effectively be used to keep the witness on a very short rein. If it had been necessary to deal with these topics it might have been done on the following lines.

Q   As a director of the parent company you were an authorised signatory of parent company cheques weren't you?
Q   Were you also entitled to sign cheques for A company during the period we are concerned with in this case?
Q   Who was the cashier during this time?
Q   Was it part of her duty to draw up cheques for cash?
Q   When you were there were you usually asked to sign those cheques?
Q   Was there a security officer there during this period?
Q   Did he become a signatory of A company cheques?
Q   Were there occasions when you were there when he signed cheques and you did not?
Q   When you were not there, he then used to sign?
Q   That was the purpose of making him a signatory wasn't it?

The actual examination continued on the same general lines until the examiner reached at length the evidence which bore directly on the issue in the case.

Q   Now I want to turn to another topic, and that is this: you know of course what is alleged in this case. If you did not at the start of the case, you must know now. As far as you were concerned, was there any fiddle or fraud such as has been described in this case?

A No.

Note.
The advocate has made a little speech, which is strictly not permitted. None the less this kind of comment is often slipped into questioning and is designed to direct the tribunal to a particular line of thought. It is better if you avoid comment like this; there are many judges who would intervene and criticise which would, in any event, undermine the purpose of the comment. If the circumstances were such that you felt justified in making a comment in your question you should make sure that it is sound and realistic. In this instance it must have struck the jury as very odd that they were being told that this defendant did not know what was being alleged against him at the start of the case.

The examiner continued:

Q Or any sort of fiddle or fraud?
A No.
Q If it is said that if a fraud or fiddle of the sort were carried out by dishonest lorry drivers from A company or dishonest weighbridge people at B company, where a cheque payment is needed, it would need someone like you in order to syphon some of the money off to pay the dishonest lorry drivers and weighbridge men? You follow the argument?
A Yes.
Q Supposing there was such a fraud being worked, would it need someone like you to syphon off the money, or could they get their ill-gotten gains in some other way?
A No money could be syphoned off.
Q Why do you say that?
A Because the controls on this money were too strict.
Q Supposing that they did it, just theorising, how could they get their unjust reward?
A Well, the only way is, if there was a fiddle or fraud as you say, like this, the only possible way, as I see it, would be that the amount of overweight that had been received, or got, or whatever you like to say, would have had to have been sold. Sold off. They would have had to go out early in the morning, or something like that, and sold off, because no way could you get money out of our company.
Q So far as you were aware, was anything like that being done?
A No, no.

Q Again, supposing that a fiddle or fraud such as alleged by the prosecution were done with your connivance, was somebody in your position able to sign cheques and so forth? Would you in your position have been gaining anything by the fraud?

A No.

Note.

These questions go to the heart of the defence. All that the examiner wanted was for the witness to be able to deny convincingly that he was concerned in the fraud. The defence argument was that if the witness had been involved, as paymaster, it would have meant that he was drawing cheques payable to cash and he could only have done that with the knowledge of the cashier or the security officer. Neither had been charged with any offence because there was no evidence that they connived at the fraud. It was also part of the defence that as the payment by B company to A company was made by cheque, and the alleged purpose of the fraud was to benefit A company's receipts, the witness would not be deriving a personal benefit by participating in the fraud. The prosecution argument was that there was something in the region of £2.5 million drawn in cash for legitimate purposes in the course of a year at A company. It would therefore have been possible for the witness, who was a director of the company, to instruct the cashier to draw cheques to cash, giving some feasible reason for the drawings; and as the cash drawings were so large they would be easy to hide. As to benefit, the prosecution could prove that the A company was carrying a very large overdraft and a motive for the fraud could well have been to benefit the company by making it appear that it was doing better than it really was. When you appreciate these competing arguments you will see that the questions asked by the examiner were not sufficiently well thought out to present the witness in the best light. A better line of questions might have been as follows:

Q The prosecution allege that the lorry drivers and the weighbridge men were defrauding B company by pretending that A company had delivered to B company more metal than had been delivered. You understand that to be the allegation don't you?

Q Did you at the time have any idea that such a fraud was being committed?

Q The implication of the prosecution case is that you organised the alleged fraud. Did you organise such a fraud?

Q Did the Company have an overdraft?

Q For how long had it carried an overdraft?

Q What was the highest figure of the overdraft during the year in question? Please look at the bank statements to refresh your memory.

Q Did you as a director of the parent company have any undue concern at the size of the overdraft?

Q Was the profitability of A company even on the agenda for discussion or review by the management?

Q You have already told us that the cashier was generally responsible for drawing cheques when cash was needed, and that you usually signed them if you were there. Did you ever draw a cheque to cash, and sign it without telling the cashier?

Q Did you ever make an entry in the cash book yourself? Just look at the cash book.

Q Do you recognise the writing in the cash book?

Q Whose is it?

Q Is the detail of every cheque drawn on the company entered in that cash book?

Q Is that cash book inspected during the year by the company auditors?

Q Do they have an obligation to draw attention to any unexplained or apparently irregular entries?

Q Were any such irregularities drawn to your attention by the auditors?

Q I suppose it might be alleged that you asked the cashier on numerous occasions to draw a cheque to cash and gave her an untrue reason for the drawing which would pass unnoticed by the auditors when they saw it in the book. Did you do any such thing?

Q As you have said the cashier normally drew up the cheques ready for you to sign. Do you ever remember drawing a company cheque yourself rather than leaving it to her to do so?

Q At all events it would have been a very unusual occurrence?

Q If a dishonest driver who had the connivance of the weighbridge men wanted to make some extra money for himself would it be possible for him to sell off part of the load after he left A company and before he reached B company?

Q If that was happening would you expect to be told of it by the drivers?

Q Did it in any way come to your knowledge that that was happening?

Q I ask you again, did you have anything whatsoever to do with the fraud that is alleged or with any fraud?

You will notice how, in these questions, there is a combination of permissible leading and pointed non-leading questions. Each important aspect of the defence and prosecution case is dealt with step by step. The judge and jury can follow each point without difficulty. There is an obvious argument which informs the questions. The prospect of the witness giving away any damaging or potentially damaging information is minimised. The actual examination continued much as follows:

Q   Do you know what the issued shares, the total value of the issued shares, of the parent company is?
A   No, not off-hand I don't. I know there are 15 million shares. I don't know whether they were all issued or not.
Q   Approximately how many of those issued shares did you hold at the time in question?
A   The same as I hold now, 150 something thousand. Just over 150,000.
Q   Was there a time when you once held 180,000?
A   No.
Q   Because I think you are shown on some document ...
A   No. I think you will find what happened, the original issue was I think, my original issue was about 118,000, and then about, I cannot remember how many years ago, we had an issue of one for every five held. That brought it up to my present holding.
Q   That is 150 plus?
A   Yes, whatever is in the latest accounts.

Note.

The point which the examiner was approaching was that the witness had nothing to gain personally by the fraud. As we have seen these questions were essentially irrelevant; but what made things worse was that the witness was allowed to take control. The examiner had it in mind that there was a document which appeared to contradict what the witness was saying. He did not have it at his fingertips, and when the witness contradicted his recollection of what the document said, he unwisely let the matter drop. As a result the opening questions in cross-examination of the witness went as follows:

Q   Mr Z why did you deny that you had ever held more than 153,000 shares?
A   Because it's the truth.
Q   Is it?
A   As far as I know, yes.
Q   Would you look please at page 71 in bundle A. Do you see that?
A   Yes.
Q   It shows that you were holding 183,498 shares, doesn't it?

A   Yes.
Q   Were you?

The witness then went into a long unconvincing explanation which was shown to be contradictory to another part of the same document. In the result the witness was severely damaged in his credibility at the outset of his cross-examination. That could have been avoided had the examiner not made the mistakes which have been pointed out.

Every witness poses individual problems to the examiner, but they can all be overcome by the application of the general principles of examination which have been illustrated in this chapter. Sufficient has been said of the importance of clarity of thought in the framing of questions; of the necessity for precise questions to be asked which demand the answer which is required; of the methods by which a witness should be kept under control; of the necessity for order in the questioning: of the use of simple language easily and invariably understood by the witness; and above all of knowing your case and the part that the witness plays in it, down to the last detail. I want to conclude this chapter with a word or two about the manner in which examination ought to be conducted.

You should always bear in mind that a prerequisite of persuading a tribunal to come to a decision in your favour is to secure its close attention. This means that you must always strive to catch and retain the interest of your judges. It was that characteristic which Ben Jonson seized on in his tribute to the speaking of Francis Bacon: 'Yet there hapn'd, in my time, one noble speaker, who was full of gravity in his speaking. His language (where he could spare, or pass by a jest), was nobly censorious. No man ever spoke more neatly, more presly, more weightily, or suffered less emptiness, less idleness, in what he uttered. No member of his speech but consisted of the own graces: his hearers could not cough or look aside from him without loss. He commanded where he spoke: and had his judges angry and pleased at his devotion. No man had their affections more in his power. The fear of every man that heard him was lest he should make an end.'

You should strive to interest the court not only in what you have to say in your speech, but also in what your witnesses have to say. You might think that the advocate has little to do in this respect because what the witness has to say is either interesting or not depending on the facts to which he testifies: but the reality is that you may often, by skilfully taking the witness to the points in issue, and by making your manner cheerful and helpful elicit the evidence with clarity and humour. Good humour creates an agreeable atmosphere in court which is often conducive to the acceptance of the points which you are making. I am referring here to simple unaffected good humour and not wit, and certainly not flippancy. Wit however, when apposite, can be a formidable influence in your advocacy. An example of the apt remark follows. Its effect on the jury was to put the advocate on good terms with them and contributed significantly to the defendant's acquittal. The defendant in a case of dangerous driving was being examined. He was explaining that he was driving an ice-cream van down a very steep hill and his case was that his brakes had suddenly failed. He had described how he had been driving along in a perfectly normal manner, with his mate sitting on the refrigerator beside him, when he came to the hill and began to go down it. He described in over-emphatic terms his horror at finding his brakes did not work. He looked to his right and to his left, there was a precipice on either side, in front there was a vehicle coming towards him, he did not know what to do, he thought of his wife and children. At this point the judge intervened, apparently to deflect the witness from the melodramatic account he was giving; 'What was your companion doing?' The witness was stopped in his tracks, nonplussed. His advocate came to his rescue; 'I have no doubt, your honour, that he was keeping cool.'

I shall conclude this chapter with a demonstration of how the methods of questioning just illustrated may be adopted in an everyday type of case.

The defendant was charged with wounding with intent contrary to s. 18 of the Offences Against the Person Act 1861.

It was alleged that the defendant had fired a gun at a man on a motor cycle and had wounded him in the leg. The witness, whose statement is given below, saw the incident and purported to have recognised the defendant as the assailant. The issues in the case were (a) whether the incident had occurred, and (b) if so, whether the witness had or had not correctly identified the defendant as the assailant.

Here is a possible examination in chief and a cross-examination of an eye-witness to the alleged offence. In both illustrations I have left the answers to the questions to be imagined.

Statement of Celia Isee

Age. Over 21.

This statement consisting of four pages each signed by me is true to the best of my knowledge and belief and I make it knowing that if it is tendered in evidence, I shall be liable to prosecution if I have wilfully stated in it anything which I know to be false or do not believe to be true.

Dated 29 February 1994.

Note The Statement though signed by the witness has not been witnessed as it ought to have been.

I live at the address overleaf.

At about 5.18 p.m. on Saturday 29 February 1994 I took my dog for a walk.

I had got to the position by the round pond at the junction of Emu Street and Toggle Terrace when I saw a motor cycle and driver indicate and then turn right into Toggle Terrace after coming along Emu Street from the direction of Longdrive Road.

Immediately afterwards a light blue old type Vauxhall Cavalier turned into Toggle Terrace right behind the motor cycle.

I saw that the person driving the Vauxhall was a person I know to be Waldo Emerson, who I have known to look at for a number of years.

At this point I was about twenty feet away from Emerson with a clear unrestricted view. It was still light. I was aware of another person in the passenger seat but I did not see him and I have no idea what he looked like. Waldo Emerson had got dark brown wavy hair which was quite long. I do not think that it was quite onto his shoulder.

The Vauxhall drew to a halt and Emerson opened the driver's side window. The motorcyclist, who was wearing a crash helmet and a brown leather jacket, looked back and stopped. Emerson stuck his head out of the car. I heard somebody say 'Have you got a problem?' I do not know who said it.

Emerson then reversed the car back to the end of the street with the motorcyclist now being about 12–15 feet in front of the car. I saw Emerson open the car door and I noticed that he pulled out a long dark object. As soon as I saw this object I thought 'He's pulling a gun out'.

I saw Emerson point the gun at the motorcyclist and fire it. There was a very loud bang. The motorcyclist started to drive off. He drove up to the junction with Arnold Avenue and along the side of the round pond up to Longdrive Road. He then turned right as if going towards the town.

As soon as Emerson fired the gun he pulled it back into the car. He had it in his right hand. He pulled the door to and drove up to the junction of

Emu Street and Dog Lane. He turned left into Anselm Way as if going towards Becket Lane.

I would describe the gun as being between 12 and 18 inches long. I can remember seeing the flash at the end of the barrel as the gun fired.

I can remember a woman came out of one of the houses on Toggle Terrace after the gun had gone off. The whole incident lasted a short time.

I felt very shocked by the incident. Only a few moments before two young boys had been on the side of the round pond. My heart was going very fast.

I ran back to my house and telephoned the police. I do not think anyone else was close by during the incident. I cannot remember seeing anyone else there.

I did not see the passenger in the Vauxhall take any part in the incident.

When preparing the examination in chief of this witness a number of useful points will be apparent:

(a)   Although the statement has been taken by someone in the CPS, something of the personality of the witness peeps through. It is plain that she is observant of detail and is careful before committing herself to categorical statement: 'I was aware of another person in the passenger seat but I did not see him and I have no idea what he looked like'; 'I noticed that he pulled out a long dark object. As soon as I saw this object I thought ''He's pulling a gun out'''.

(b)   This latter observation is particularly revealing because it acutely distinguishes between actually seeing from the first that it was a gun and the inference that it was a gun. So the examiner may assume that the witness has a clear mind and is likely to be accurate in recall. It will also be noticed that she gives an exact time, to the minute. It is therefore evident that although she does not state it she had a reason for noticing the time when she went out for a walk. That time may be of significance because at the time of the incident she says that it was still light. Let us suppose that lighting-up time was 5.35 p.m. How long was she walking with the dog from setting out to the time of the incident? This may be a potentially vulnerable point in her evidence. You will want to find out in chief whether any of the vehicles had their lights on.

(c)   There are a number of different streets mentioned and it will be advisable to have at least a sketch plan to show the lay out of the neighbourhood. It will also allow the witness to get her bearings. Get her to make a sketch plan early on, or if you have a scale plan introduce it early. It will also be a good opportunity to allow the witness to get used to the courtroom atmosphere before coming to the vital parts of her evidence.

(d)   There are some potentially difficult points to surmount. They will need careful thought before the examination begins. How did she know Emerson to look at for a number of years? Has he a bad character, and is he therefore well-known? You will have to be careful not to adduce inadmissible evidence accidentally.

Why does she say that Emerson 'had got' dark brown wavy hair? Has he recenty changed his hair colour and style? If so it may show that the witness has seen him *since* the incident and before making the statement But the statement is dated the same day as the incident. There may be absolutely nothing in the point; but it is well to be alert to it. We shall look at it again when it comes to cross-examination. My reason for drawing attention to what may seem at first sight to be an extremely little point is because it is in little points that people give themselves away unconsciously.

(e)   Whenever you begin an examination in chief, note the date when the statement was made. You may be able to use the statement as a memory refreshing document if it was sufficiently contemporaneous.

Here is a line of questioning which might be followed with this witness:

Q   What is your full name?
Q   How close do you live to the round pond?
Q   Please look at this plan. Show us where you live.
Q   Where is the round pond?
Q   Please will you write in the following roads: Emu Street; Toggle Terrace; Anselm Way; Becket Lane and Dog Lane.
Q   In February of last year were you in the habit of walking your dog?
Q   Was there an occasion when something unusual occurred? Do you happen to remember the date?
Q   Was it morning or afternoon?
Q   Can you by chance remember the time at which you left your house?
Q   How is it that you remember the time so exactly?
Q   Where were you approximately when the incident occurred?
Q   About how long after leaving your house was this?
Q   How busy with traffic was Emu Street and Toggle Terrace?
Q   Was your dog on or off the lead?

Q When you were near the round pond did you see anyone on foot or anyone in or on a vehicle?

Q How many vehicles did you see in all?

Q Can you describe each of those vehicles?

Q How was the motorcyclist dressed?

Q Can you give any description of the rider's face?

Q How many people were in the Vauxhall?

Q Where were you standing when you first saw the Vauxhall?

Q How close were you when that car passed you?

Q Who sat nearer you? Driver or passenger?

Q For how long was the driver in your sight as the car approached?

Q Was there any reason why you particularly noticed the driver?

Q How recently had you seen him before?

Q Had you ever spoken to him?

Q On this occasion did you recognise him before or after he had passed you?

Q At about what speed was the car travelling?

Q Was the view you had of his face in profile, or full face or what?

Q Was there anything particular by which you recognised him?

Q Apart from greeting him, had you ever spoken to him before?

Q On how many occasions do you think that you have seen him in the street in the last year or so?

Q When you saw him on this occasion was there anything in your line of vision?

Q Did you notice the colour of his hair?

Q Did you notice the length of his hair?

Q What was the weather like?

Q How low was the sun?

Q Is there anything by which you remember that?

Q Are there any street lamps just there?

Q Were they lit or unlit?

Q Did any of the vehicles have their lights on that you remember?

Q Where did the Vauxhall go after passing you?

Q Can you just show us on the plan where it stopped?

Q And where were you at this time?

Q Which of the car doors was nearest to you?

Q Was your view at all restricted?

Q Where was the motorcyclist now?

Q Was there any reason that you could see why he stopped?

Q How far was the rider from the car?

Q Did you notice whether the Vauxhall driver's window was up or down?

Q Was there any particular reason why you noticed that it was down?

Q When he stuck his head out, did you hear anything?

Q Are you able to say who said that?

Q Can you remember the tone of voice?

Q Did the car remain where it was?

Q How far did it reverse?

Q Did it stop or go on?

Q Where was the cyclist?

Q Were the doors of the car open or closed?

Q When the driver's door was opened what, if anything, did the driver do?

Q From where did the long object come?

Q What made you think it was a gun rather than, say, a stick?

Q How was he holding it? With one or two hands?

Q Where was the gun pointing?

Q Did you hear or see anything at that moment?

Q Did anything happen which made you think that anyone else had heard the bang?

Q Please will you mark on the plan which house that was?

Q After the flash and the bang, what happened to the cyclist?

Q What happened to the car?

Q What did you do?

Q During the incident did you see anyone else other than the people you have described?

Notes.

(1)   This examination in chief allows the witness to give her account in her own words without any significant leading questions, even on matters not directly in dispute. Nonetheless the witness is held under tight control. There are very few questions of the 'what happened next' variety.

(2)   Each topic is dealt with thoroughly before passing to the next.

(3)   Possible vulnerable points are dealt with cautiously or, in two instances, not at all.

It will be more convenient for the reader if I demonstrate a possible cross-examination here, rather than in Chapter 6 on cross-examination.

The task of cross-examining this witness effectively is quite formidable. If she has come up to proof she will have created a strong impression of truthfulness on the jury. Although the prosecution are put to proof that the incident occurred, it is likely to be a fruitless task to attempt to show that this witness is lying.

The objective of cross-examination is therefore to show that she is mistaken in her identification. Your instructions are that it was not the defendant who was there at the scene.

For these purposes I shall proceed on the basis that there is very little information available from the defendant's instructions with which to confront the witness. Obviously, when taking instructions you would explore whether the defendant had any brothers who resembled him; or whether he had ever been mistaken for someone else.

It would be of great value if, before cross-examining, you could go to the scene of the incident to spy out the lie of the land. But assume in this case that nothing came of it.

What are the points which should be attacked?

(a)   There was no identification parade. If the witness was wrong in her purported identification at the scene, she is wrong now. There has been nothing by which to measure her accuracy.

(b)   The exact time at which she set out for her walk takes her very close to sunset and lighting-up time. The longer you can establish that she was walking before the incident, the less light there must have been to make the identification. It is likely that you will have amongst the unused material the time at which her call to the police was logged. If it has not been disclosed you should pursue it. It will enable you to test the accuracy of her recollection by fixed times.

(c)   Although the evidence does not fall into the fleeting glance category, there is no doubt that the conditions in which the identification was made were far from ideal. The witness has said that she was very shocked by the incident. She was unable to describe at all the passenger sitting beside the driver. She does not specifically say whether it was a man or a woman. She seems to have made an assumption that it was a man.

In addition, although this is a purported recognition case, the circumstances in which the witness knew the defendant are somewhat vague.

(d)   There may be something in the point mentioned earlier about the use of the phrase 'had got dark brown wavy hair'. The person who took the statement has not witnessed the witness's signature. A departure from the rules.

The cross-examination might go like this:

Q You were never asked to test your identification by an identity parade were you?

Q How often do you say that you had seen Mr Emerson in the course of the year before this incident?

Q On none of those three occasions did you speak to him, did you?

Q Were you on the same side of the road on any of those occasions?

Q How long do you say his hair was on the first occasion?

Q How long on the second?

Q How long on the third?

Q What about the colour of his hair?

Q Was it different on any of those occasions?

Q Is it different now compared with any other time when you have seen him?

Q Why do you say in your statement that he had got dark brown wavy hair?

Q Did you mean to imply that at other times when you have seen him his hair appeared different?

Q Then please explain why you used that phrase.

Q You would agree, I suppose, that young men with long hair often look alike?

Q You said a few minutes ago that there was no particular feature by which you recognised the defendant, didn't you?

Q You would agree, would you not, with the common observation that many people have look-a-likes?

Q You would agree that your opportunity to take in what was happening was very short?

Q You regularly walk your dog don't you?

Q Do you usually go the same route?

Q How long do you usually walk for?

Q It's hardly worth going out for under half an hour is it?

Q That evening did you walk on the common as usual?

Q The common is opposite the round pond isn't it?

Q You were returning from the common when this incident occurred weren't you?

Q By the time you reached the road it was practically dark wasn't it?

Q By then on your account you had been walking for about 25 minutes hadn't you?

Q You agree that the round pond is about two minutes from your house?

Q You have agreed already that you usually walked for about 30 minutes or more?

Q Do you still deny that it was nearly dark by the time you reached the road?

Q When you saw the car coming towards you did it have its headlights on?

Q If they might have been, might you have been dazzled by them?

Q You would agree that if you were dazzled by them it would make any identification of the driver extremely difficult? If not impossible?

Q And you agree that you were quite unable to describe the passenger?

Q You cannot describe that person's clothes? Or even whether it was a man, a woman or a child?

Q Was that because it was too dark to see?

Q How long were you out that evening from the time you left your house to the time you phoned the police?

Q Try and remember.

Q You can work it out roughly can't you?

Q Tell us to the nearest few minutes.

Q You say about 29 minutes, do you?

Q If you left, as you say, at 5.18 you must have been on the phone to the police at about 5.48 mustn't you?

Q Did you know that the police logged your call at five minutes past six?

Q The truth is that when you made your purported identification it was almost dark?

I have tried in this simulated cross-examination to show how the skilful use of limited information can disable a witness. I deliberately did not utilise all the vulnerable points of attack to which I referred earlier. This is true to life. If you are doing well do not drag in points which may not be so productive or which might weaken the pressure on the witness. When the witness gives you an opportunity, follow it up, but stop when you have got what you want. The one strong point that you have here is the time when the police logged the phone call, which taken together with the time of leaving the house enables the cross-examiner to lead up to a convincing climax. You will find, surprisingly often, that even where you have a weak case there either is, or you can elicit, valuable information with which you can confront the witness.

Six

Cross-examination

Carson: What is the direction of current dramatic taste?

W. S. Gilbert: In the direction of musical comedy, in which half a dozen irresponsible comedians are turned loose to do on the stage as they please.

Carson: Will you mention one of them?

W. S. Gilbert: Oh there are plenty of them!

Carson: I wish you would mention one?

W. S. Gilbert: Well, take the pantomime at Drury Lane theatre with the great Dan Leno.

Carson: But that only goes on for a short time of the year?

W. S. Gilbert: It goes on for a long time in the evening.

Carson: Do you really describe a pantomime as bad musical comedy?

W. S. Gilbert: No, but I would describe a bad musical comedy as a pantomime.

Carson: Give me the name of one bad musical comedy?

W. S. Gilbert: I would say such a piece as 'The Circus Girl'.

Carson: Would you call it a bad musical comedy?

W. S. Gilbert: I would call it bad, I believe the manager calls it musical comedy.

(W. S. Gilbert, V The Era)

The purposes of cross-examination are to destroy or weaken the evidence of your opponent's witnesses, or to undermine their credibility. In addition cross-examination should be used to elicit favourable evidence, and must be used to put your case to the witnesses for the other side.

The foundation of all effective cross-examination is to base your questions on the lines of an argument; each question being a discrete step in the argument. Sometimes it is necessary to disguise the form of the argument for tactical reasons, but the questions put by the cross-examiner will none the less be dictated by the argument. As will be illustrated in this chapter every effective cross-examination follows this basic rule, and you should acquire the habit of adhering to it on all occasions.

The tools for cross-examination were well described by Munkman in his *The Technique of Advocacy* (Stevens and Sons Ltd, 1951 p. 68 *et seq*) where he designated names to types of questions; probing, insinuation and confrontation. The advantage of distinguishing these different types of question is that it enables you to appreciate more easily which type of question is being used when it is heard or read and is therefore a valuable aid to analysis.

A probing question is one which is designed to elicit information and to tie the witness down to a definite account of events. An example may be given from the trial of Dickman (*Notable British Trial Series,* p. 113). Tindal Atkinson is opening his cross-examination of the defendant.

Q   You say you knew the deceased man?
A   I knew the deceased man; but if I had been asked off-hand what his name was, I could not have told you.
Q   Did you know his name?
A   No; if any one had said to me 'Do you know Nisbet?' after a description, I would have known the man.
Q   I do not understand you. Did you know his name or did you not?
A   Yes; but if I had been asked off-hand, I would not be able to call that man Nisbet.
Q   But you knew his name was Nisbet?
A   Yes.
Q   [The Judge] You knew him and you knew his name?
A   Yes, if it had been mentioned to me.
Q   [Tindal Atkinson] I do not quite understand that. Did you know his name independently at that time of anybody telling it to you?
A   No, he was not an individual who was in my mind at all.

Q I did not ask you that. It is a very plain question. Did you know this man by name?

A Yes, I did know him by name.

Q On the 18th of March did you know this man by name?

A I did.

Q [The Judge] And by sight?

A By sight. I knew he was a Quaysider.

Q [Tindal Atkinson] Did you know what he was?

A I knew he was a clerk on the quay, but whom he was employed with or where he was employed I did not know.

Q Did you know he was clerk and book keeper to a colliery company?

A No I did not. Whether he was with a firm of merchants or shipbrokers or general dealers, or anything like that, I was not aware.

Q You have been connected with a colliery?

A Yes.

Q Do you know that wages are paid once a fortnight?

A I do.

Q Do you know that they are usually paid on Friday?

A Yes.

Q Do you know that wages are usually taken from the place of business in Newcastle to the collieries in the neighbourhood of Newcastle?

A No, I could not say that — in fact to any particular colliery.

Q Do you know that money has been brought?

A It may have been.

Q Money has to be drawn from the Bank?

A Yes in my own case I always got the money at the bank at Morpeth.

Q Wherever the bank is, and wherever the bank account is kept, the cheque would have to be drawn?

A And cashed.

Q And the money obtained?

A Yes.

Q And carried by someone?

A Yes.

Q To the colliery where the wages had to be paid?

A Yes.

Q You knew that?

A Yes, I had done the same business myself.

Q I suppose you know that they are usually carried in a bag of some sort?

A Yes.

Q   A leather bag?
Q   I could not say whether it was leather, but cash bags are usually
      leather.

Notes.

(1)   The questioner asks these probing questions until he elicits a
clear answer. He is not put off by vague or prevaricating answers. You
should acquire the habit of pressing the simple pointed question until you
compel the witness to answer it. The failure to do this is, probably, the
most common fault in cross-examination.

(2)   Each topic is dealt with completely before passing to the next.

(3)   Dickman was charged with murder. It was alleged that he had
killed Nisbet on a train. The motive was said to be robbery. Nisbet was
carrying the wages from the bank to the colliery. The murder had
evidently been carefully planned by someone who must have known
Nisbet, known that he took wages to the colliery every fortnight, and
always took that particular train. The questions quoted above are based
on the following argument. The fact that he knew Nisbet by name makes
it more probable that he knew that he was a clerk among whose duties it
was to carry the wages. The fact that he knew very well the system by
which colliery workers were paid fortnightly and the fact that he knew
the wages were usually carried in a leather bag means that he had the
knowledge that the murderer must have had.

You will notice how the examiner has arranged these topics. Name
first and employment second. He knows that he can compel the witness
to admit that he knew Nisbet's name, but that he has no material
to establish that he knew precisely what his employment was; he
therefore places that topic very briefly between the facts which he can
establish, the knowing of Nisbet's name and knowing the system by
which wages were paid. Even though he has got a negative answer to
whether the defendant had a precise knowledge of Nisbet's employment
the denial is much weakened by forcing admissions on the other facts.
This order of questions is also part of the logical consistency of the
argument.

(4)   A characteristic of effective examination is the short pointed
question which compels the witness to answer with precision or
otherwise appear to dodge and weave away from it. Look how effective
these questions are. Did you know his name or did you not? But you knew
his name was Nisbet? Did you know this man by name? On the 18th of
March did you know this man by name?

Consider another illustration. Helen Duncan was tried, together with others, for pretending that she was able to conjure up spirits from the dead contrary to s. 4 of the Witchcraft Act 1735. Mr Homer, a co-defendant, gave evidence of the appearance of materialised forms at seances at which he assisted, including one on 19 January 1944. (The extract is taken from *Notable Cross-Examinations* by E. W. Fordham, p. 168.) Mr John Maude KC cross-examined him as follows:

Q   Where have you observed Albert [the spirit guide] from?
A   The front seat.
Q   Why did you always sit in the front seat?
A   To attend to Mrs Duncan when she comes out of the cabinet, to put her in my seat.
Q   How many times have you seen Albert?
A   Many times.
Q   Have you seen Albert twenty times?
A   Yes.
Q   How big a beard has he got?
A   Not a thick growth, but [pointing] from here to there.
Q   What happens when you get beyond that? Is there white stuff round it?
A   Just the face.
Q   What happens outside the beard?
A   A spirit shroud.
Q   Is it a white thing?
A   An ectoplasmic shroud.
Q   Is it identical with what you would get if somebody had a white cloth over their head hanging down?
A   No Sir.
Q   What is the difference?
A   It is a very white and fine substance.
Q   What is the difference between that and butter muslin?
A   I would not call it butter muslin.
Q   Does it look very like butter muslin?
A   Very like.
Q   Is there anything else it looks more like?
A   No.
Q   Then are we not right it looks very like a shroud made of butter muslin?
A   Yes.

These are typical of probing questions designed to elicit a definite account from the witness and to detect and expose inherent weaknesses in the account he has given.

Notes.

(1)   Who, what, why, when, where, and how are characteristic probing questions.

(2)   The argument which lies behind these questions is that there is no difference between what the witness is pleased to call 'a spirit shroud' and somebody with butter muslin over his head; and the aim is to contrast a natural, commonsense explanation with the far-fetched.

(3)   The order of the questions is logical. He establishes his point in the following steps. The witness has seen Albert many times. He has had the best possible view. He is able to describe the size of his beard. How then does he describe the shroud? How is it distinguishable from butter muslin? He has established that there is no foundation for the bland assertion that there was a 'spirit shroud'.

(4)   Is there anything else it looks more like?' is designed to prevent the witness from resiling from the answers he has so far given.

Skilful questioning should compel the witness to concede an exact position. What is the difference between the shroud and butter muslin is a good probing question. It makes the witness commit himself; makes him justify a previous vague undetailed answer. The technique of this type of question depends on the use of contrast.

One further illustration of the use of probing questions is taken from the 'Tichborne Claimants' case. The real heir to the family fortune was Sir Roger Tichborne. He was on board the *Bella* in 1854, was shipwrecked and was drowned. In 1865 a butcher of Wagga Wagga, in Australia, assumed the title and claimed the estates. There were two actions. The first was an action for ejectment. At an early stage it was placed in the hands of Chancery Counsel, and later in those of the Attorney General, Sir John Coleridge.

In the *Reminiscencies of Sir Henry Hawkins* (Baron Brampton, vol. 1, p. 310), Hawkins says that Chancery Counsel examined on these lines:

Q   Will you swear, sir, that you were on board the Bella?
A   I will.
Q   Let me make a note of that. Do you swear you were picked up and taken to Australia?

A I do sir.
Q Stop. Let me make a note of that.

At last, however, Hawkins was entrusted with the case, as he should have been at first because he was the most able cross-examiner of his day. He excelled at probing.

One of the witnesses whom Hawkins had to examine was an old servant of the Tichborne's called Bogle. Hawkins relates (*loc. cit.* p. 321): 'Bogle had sworn that Sir Roger had no tattoo marks when he left England. In point of fact he had. But Bogle had to fit him to the claimant who had tattoo marks of a very different kind from Roger's. The claimant had removed his and therefore was presented to the court without any.' Unlike the Chancery barrister who would have been content to ask him 'You swear Roger had no tattoo marks? Very well, let me write that down', Hawkins questioned him as follows:

Q How do you know Roger had no tattoo marks?
A I saw his arms on three occasions.
[Hawkins then asked in quick succession, when, where, and in what circumstances.]
Q The sleeves, how were they?
A Loose.
Q How came you to see his naked arms?
A He was rubbing one of them like this.
Q What did he rub for?
A I thought he'd got a flea.
Q Did you see it?
A No, of course.
Q Where was it?
A Just there.
Q What time was this?
A Ten minutes past eleven.
Q That's the first occasion: come to the second.
A Just the same.
Q Same time?
A Yes.
Q Did he always put his hand inside his sleeve to rub?
A I don't know.
Q But I want to know.
A If your shirt was unbuttoned Mr Hawkins, and you was rubbing your arm, you would draw up your sleeve.

Q Never mind what I should do; I want to know what you saw.
A The same as before.
Q A flea?
A I suppose.
Q But did you see him?
A I told you Mr Hawkins, I did not.
Q Excuse me, that was on the first occasion.
A Well, this was the same.
Q Same flea?
A I suppose.
Q Same time — ten minutes past eleven?
A Yes.
Q Then all I can say is, he must have been a very punctual old flea.

Notes.

(1)   The characteristic of this examination is that Hawkins was, by the use of probing questions, compelling the witness to invent his evidence. As Hawkins knew that he was lying he could safely press him without fear of getting an unfavourable answer which he could not deal with. You will notice that he forces the witness into giving a positive answer to each question before passing to the next. He only suggests an answer to the witness when he wants the witness to give that answer. As the witness is not very intelligent he cannot think quickly enough to invent a plausible story, particularly as Hawkins would have asked these questions very rapidly.

(2)   What time was this?, was a resourceful question, though somewhat risky. The witness would have gained some sympathy if he had said 'How can you possibly expect me to remember the time at which he scratched his arm?' Whether you risk such a question is a matter of practical judgment. I suppose that Hawkins was ready for such an answer, and would have questioned along the following lines: You are saying that you remember this exceedingly trivial incident, you say you remember when and where it took place; it is therefore not unreasonable to expect you to remember the time. His object is to ridicule the evidence given by the witness.

(3)   When the witness tries to draw Hawkins into a personal argument Hawkins brings him straight back to the point. Never get embroiled in a personal argument with the witness.

The next type of question to consider is insinuation, which can be used effectively for many purposes. It is certainly the best method of putting your case to the witness. It is a fundamental rule of cross-examination that you must give the witness an opportunity of dealing with the case you are putting if his account is different from yours. If the witness says that your client was in Chancery Lane at 3 p.m. on Saturday, and your case is that he was there on Friday at 2 p.m. you must challenge the witness's evidence. As a general rule the way to put your case is to ask questions which reveal the account your witness will give. It is not usually sufficient simply to say 'you are wrong' or the defendant 'did not do such and such'. This only results in the 'he did' — 'no he didn't' type of exchange. Needless to say this will do no good and may serve only to rub in the case against you. The way to put a coherent alternative account is as follows:

Q What were you doing in Chancery Lane when you saw the defendant?

A I was doing some shopping.

Q Did you go to any shops in Chancery Lane?

A Yes, I did.

Q Which particular shops did you go to?

A I went to the chemist and to Ede & Ravenscroft.

Q You went into Ede & Ravenscroft at about 2 o'clock didn't you?

A No. I would say it was about 3 o'clock.

Q Did you buy a blue bag?

A Yes, I did.

Q Were you served by a man with a large birthmark on the right side of his face?

A Yes, I was.

Q When he had served you did he say he was going to a late lunch?

A Yes, I believe he did.

Q Does that remind you that it was nearer 2 than 3 o'clock when you went into that shop?

A Well, it might have been.

Q Are you aware that Ede & Ravenscroft are closed on Saturdays?

A No, I was not.

Q If they are closed on Saturdays would you concede that it must have been Friday when you bought the blue bag?

A Yes, if they are closed on Saturdays, I must be mistaken.

Notes.

In this imaginary cross-examination the examiner was in the happy position of having good information at his disposal. He has used it to best effect, by putting step by step the case he is advancing; each question presses for an exact answer.

(1)   The argument is that the witness must be mistaken because the shop is closed on Saturdays and the assistant with whom he dealt has been traced and will say that he went to lunch at about 2 p.m. immediately after serving the witness.

(2)   The preliminary questions are probing. This was a wise precaution if the examiner had any reason to fear that the witness might deny going to Ede & Ravenscroft at all. He could alternatively have gone straight to the point with strong insinuation. 'On the day you saw the defendant you went to Ede & Ravenscroft didn't you?' The information he has is sufficiently strong even if the witness were to deny going to the shop. In the example, the insinuating questions are gentler and effective. Good discretion and experience in summing up a witness is what guides the examiner in deciding which approach to adopt.

(3)   Although this is an imaginary examination the information necessary to found the examination could in reality be obtained. In preparing the cross-examination the advocate would have been told that the defendant was in Chancery Lane on the Friday at about 2 p.m. and that he had seen the witness going into Ede & Ravenscroft. Enquiries will then have been made at Ede's to see if the account of the defendant could be verified. If you are not provided with the information you want, you should seek it. An example of the way in which you might think through your case so as to identify the key points has been given at the end of the chapter on preparation.

Apart from putting your case to the witnesses, insinuation can be used for a variety of different purposes. It is a very versatile type of question. It can, for example, be used as a method of presenting to the tribunal an alternative view of the facts.

In the example of the opening speech in a road accident case in the third chapter, you will remember that the suggested defence might be that the defendant had said 'I didn't see you because you were travelling so fast' and not simply 'I didn't see you'. The cross-examination of the woman driver in that case might go something like this:

Q   You were doing at least 50 m.p.h. when you rounded the bend, before the junction, weren't you?

Q   If you were, that would have been in excess of the speed-limit, wouldn't it?

Q When you rounded the bend the defendant was already coming out of the junction, wasn't he?

Q Because you were travelling so fast, you could not pull up in time could you?

Q When you spoke to the defendant after the accident, he said, 'I did not see you because you were travelling so fast', didn't he?

Notes.

(1) The examiner has built up to the crucial point along the line of his argument. If he had simply said: 'Now I want to suggest to you that the defendant said, 'I did not see you', as you say he said, but added that it was because you were travelling so fast', the impact of the question is considerably weakened.

(2) Even if the witness answers 'no' to all of these questions, the effect of them is clearly to foreshadow the defendant's case. If the defendant's case is valid, your questions will very likely shake the witness, and provide you with further ammunition. Remember, if your case is correct the witness is not telling the truth, and will know that he is lying. He will thus be under considerable pressure, least he be found out.

When you use insinuating cross-examination it often hardly matters what the answers to the questions are. If the emphasis is changed in the example given of the Chancery Lane examination you will readily see what is meant. Putting the questions in the form of strong insinuation the examination might go as follows:

Q You went into Ede & Ravenscroft on Friday didn't you?

Q You had been to the chemist immediately before hadn't you?

Q Before going to the chemist you had come from Fleet Street hadn't you?

Q You bought a blue bag from Ede's?

Q You paid £50 for it?

Q The assistant who served you had a birthmark on his face didn't he?

Q He told you he was just going to a late lunch?

Q It was just past 2 p.m. wasn't it?

Q It was Friday and not Saturday wasn't it?

Q Do you not know that Ede's is closed on Saturdays?

The impression made by a cross-examination of this sort, where the facts which inform it are so cogent, will leave the tribunal with the impression that the case being put, if proved, is irresistible. Such an examination must be based on established fact which you could prove if required.

A striking example of this sort of cross-examination is provided by Hastings' cross-examination of Sievier. The following passage is taken from E. W. Fordham's *Notable Cross-Examinations* (Constable, 1951, p. 129).

> Sievier, giving evidence on his own behalf, said: 'I do not profess to be a saint. I am a gambler. I have been a gambler all my life. Like all good sportsmen I have my ups and downs. I have owned the best horses in the world. Also the worst. I am known on every racecourse, and I gladly offer my character to the investigation of anyone who dares to question it. First and last I am an English sportsman and so I would be judged.' Turning to Sir Patrick Hastings he said 'What questions would you like to ask?'

Q You know that Mr Wooten has said that you are a blackmailer and a thief?

A Oh yes.

Q I am going to suggest that you are in every way a scoundrel and that your racing career should be ended once and for all.

A For any particular reason?

Q Many. Let us take one. Supposing an English sportsman played a game of billiards with a friend at a time when that friend was so drunk that he could not hold a cue, would it be a gross fraud to win large sums of money in such a game?

A Of course it would.

Q Do you know a man named Horne?

A I knew him well. There were two of them; two brothers. One was known as Hunting Horne, and one as Drinking Horne. When Hunting Horne was hunting he generally fell off.

[It was Drinking Horne from whom Sievier had won large sums of money one night at Monte Carlo.]

Q Did Horne pay his loss that night by cheque?

A He did.

Q If Horne was in fact so drunk as not to know what he was doing, it would be essential that he should pay his debt that night before he became sober?

A Ridiculous.

Q Who signed the cheque?

A   Horne.

Q   Who wrote out the body of the cheque?

A   I did.

Q   Was that because Horne was so drunk that he could not write it out himself?

[This Sievier indignantly denied. He also denied that at the conclusion of the evening the floor was found to be littered with uncompleted cheques, all in Sievier's handwriting, and with attempted signatures by Horne so undecipherable as to be worthless.]

Q   The next morning did Horne repudiate the cheque?

A   He did.

Q   Was that upon the ground that he had been so drunk that he did not know what he had signed.

A   It may have been.

Q   And in consequence of what had occurred that night did the British Consul at Monte Carlo direct you to leave the Principality and not come back?

Notes.

(1)   These opening questions are very bold, but are justified because of the incontrovertible evidence that he had against Sievier.

(2)   With the third question Hastings confronted the witness with exactly the case which he was going to prove against him. You can see how he framed the question in such a way that the only possible answer was the one given. If Sievier had said that it was not a gross fraud his boast of being first and last an English sportsman would have collapsed even sooner than in fact it did.

(3)   Hastings is not in the least diverted by Sievier's humorous description of the Hornes. He was probably pleased that the witness was trying to show-off because it promised that he would fall the harder.

(4)   You will have noticed how each step of the shameful events of the fraud are insinuated. Some would have put the 'who signed?' and 'who wrote?' in the form of insinuating questions, but to make them probing questions was to place the witness under even greater pressure. He would have denied the allegations if he could, and he must have been desperately tempted to risk a lie, but he feared that the cheque, at least, may have been available; and it is quite likely that Hastings had examples to confront him with if he lied.

Another use of insinuating questions is to drive the witness along so that damaging admissions are wrung from him. Take for example a passage from the cross-examination of Sir Edward Carson in the trial of Oscar Wilde. The main facts are too well-known to need explanation:

Q Had you a private room at the 'Florence'?
A Yes. I went there so that I could get a cheque cashed because the next day was a Sunday.
Q How much did you give Wood then?
A Two pounds.
Q Why?
A Because Lord Alfred Douglas asked me to be kind to him. I don't care about different social positions.
Q I suggest that you first had immoral relations with him and then gave him the money?
A It is perfectly untrue.
Q Did you consider that he had came to levy blackmail?
A I did; and I determined to face it.
Q And the way you faced it was by giving him £15 to go to America?
A That is an inaccurate description. I saw that the letters were of no value, and I gave him the money after he told me the pitiful tale about himself, foolishly perhaps, but out of pure kindness.
Q I suggest that you gave him £30. Did you give him £5 more next day?
A Yes; he told me that after paying his passage to America he would be left almost penniless. I gave him £5.
Q Had you a farewell lunch at the Florence?
A Yes.
Q It was after lunch that you gave him £5?
A Yes.
Q After Wood went to America did he ask you for money?
A No.
Q Did he call Taylor by his Christian name?
A Yes.
Q Did Wood call you Oscar?
A Yes.
Q What did you call Wood?
A His name is Alfred.
Q Didn't you call him Alf?
A No, I never use abbreviations.
Q Did you not think it a curious thing that a man with whom you were on such intimate terms should try to blackmail you?

A I thought it infamous, but Wood convinced me that such had not been his intention, though it was the intention of other people. Wood assured me that he had recovered all the letters.

Q And then Allen came with a letter, possession of which you knew he had secured improperly?

A Yes.

Q What was Allen?

A I am told he was a blackmailer.

Q Was he a blackmailer?

A I never heard of him except as a blackmailer.

Q Then you began to explain to the blackmailer what a loss your beautiful manuscript was?

A I described it as a beautiful work of art.

Q May I ask why you gave this man, who you knew was a notorious blackmailer, ten shillings?

A I gave it out of contempt.

Q Then the way you show your contempt is by paying ten shillings?

A Yes, very often.

Q I suppose he was pleased with your contempt?

A Yes, he was apparently pleased at my kindness.

Note.

In cross examining Wilde, Carson had an enormous amount of material which had been obtained by Lord Queensberry's private detectives. Throughout the cross-examination as you will see on reading it in its entirety (*Notable British Trial Series*, Ed. Montgomery Hyde, 1948) the argument of the examination was that Wilde had been associating with young men half his age, with no intellectual pretensions, whom he had showered with presents after lavishly entertaining them in private rooms at hotels. Although he denied any immorality his explanation that he simply enjoyed the company of careless youth could be shown by detailed instances of his conduct to be absurd. You will also see the order in which Carson questioned him. He dealt first with Wilde's claim that those of his writings which betrayed strong homosexual implications were simply works of art which had no immoral significance, then went on with the detailed confrontation of young man after young man with whom Wilde had associated. Eventually he took Wilde completely by surprise by asking about a man called Grainger:

Q Did you ever kiss him?

A   Oh dear no. He was a peculiarly plain boy. He was unfortunately
      extremely ugly. I pitied him for it.
Q   Was that the reason why you did not kiss him?
[The question was reiterated again and again as Wilde became
inarticulate.]

Notes.

(1)   The passage cited is an example of how the material is used by
the examiner to show the likelihood of Wilde only associating with Wood
for immoral purposes and then paying him and others off when
blackmailed; and the unlikelihood of Wilde's explanations. You will see
how the questions are designed to highlight the contrast between the
likely and the unlikely.

(2)   They are skilful questions which force Wilde to give an
explanation about Wood being innocent of an intention to blackmail, and
then immediately forcing him into an admission that he knew Allen only
as a blackmailer. This is a good example of the importance of the order in
which questions are asked. More will be said about this later in the chapter.

(3)   The absurdity of the answer which Carson has extracted, that he
paid Allen from contempt, is highlighted by sarcasm. While this is
permissible, and is sometimes a formidable weapon to exert legitimate
pressure on the witness, it should be used with caution and great
discretion. You should always bear in mind that the advocate has great
destructive power in cross-examination and that he has a moral
responsibility to use it fairly.

(4)   You should avoid the preliminary 'I suggest'. The questions
should be put directly.

The third type of question defined by Munkman is confrontation. In
the examples already cited instances of confrontation have been given.
This type of question consists in presenting the witness with an
incontrovertible fact: Ede & Ravenscroft are closed on Saturdays; Allen
was a notorious blackmailer. The confronting evidence can be placed
before the witness, and usually is, in the form of an insinuating question
as we have already seen.

Another way in which insinuating questions may be used is where you
want to draw the witness on to elaborate with circumstantial detail a lie
which he has told. Francis Wellman, in *The Art of Cross-Examination*,
4th ed., Macmillan, New York, 1946, has an excellent example of this.
Samuel Warren conducted the examination. The issue was the forgery of

a will. The witness had an indirect interest to a large amount if the will was admitted to probate.

Q [Warren (placing his thumb over the seal and holding up the will)] I understand you to say that you saw the testator sign this instrument.

A [Witness] I did.

Q And did you sign it as his request as subscribing witness?

A I did.

Q Was it sealed with red or black wax?

A With red wax.

Q Did you see him seal it with red wax?

A I did.

Q Where was the testator when he signed and sealed this will?

A In his bed.

Q Pray, how long a piece of red wax did he use?

A About three inches long.

Q And who gave the testator this piece of wax?

A I did.

Q Where did you get it?

A From the draw of his desk.

Q How did he melt that piece of wax?

A With a candle.

Q Where did the candle come from?

A I got it out of a cupboard in the room.

Q How long should you say the candle was?

A Perhaps four or five inches long.

Q Do you remember who lit the candle?

A I lit it.

Q What did you light it with?

A Why, with a match.

Q Where did you get the match?

A On the mantelshelf in the room.

[Warren] My Lord you will observe this will is sealed with a wafer.

Notes.

(1)   The argument behind this examination is that since the witness has lied in saying that he saw the testator sign the instrument he is very likely to try to substantiate the lie by circumstantial detail. You will find that one of the most effective methods of exposing an untruthful account is to probe the detail which can be expected to have accompanied the fact stated.

(2)   The insinuating question which lead the witness on — 'Was it sealed with red or black wax' — was, in one view, a trick question; and tricks should be avoided in cross-examination. This particular question may be justified because the witness was at liberty to say, had he been honest or more crafty, 'I am sorry, I can't remember, but you have it there, you tell me.' Because of the danger of such an answer it would have been more subtle in the examiner to have asked the witness whether he could remember how the will was sealed. It then might have gone something like this:

Q   How was the will sealed?
A   I don't remember, you tell me.
Q   Was it sealed when you signed it?
A   It was.
Q   If it was sealed in wax you would have seen it?
A   Yes.
Q   You might even have felt it as you signed?
A   I might have done.
Q   Do you really say that you cannot remember how this will was sealed?
A   Well now that you remind me, I think it was sealed in wax.

And the examination could then take its course, having compelled the witness to make a concession for fear that his evidence would be suspected if he were to appear unable to substantiate his presence when the will was signed, by this circumstantial detail.

(3)   The reason why the examiner went into the detail of the length of the wax and so on, was to make it impossible for the witness to resile from his account, and at the same time to show what a ready and fluent liar he was. These questions on detail need to be thought out beforehand, both their order and their range.

You may, in reading these examples, have wondered whether they have any practical value, apart from illustrating the way in which witnesses have been exposed by advocates of a past age. You may be wondering what 'modern sunbeams' can be extracted from these 'ancient cucumbers'. The answer which I would emphatically give is that these examples can be used as models for cross-examination whenever a similar type of examination is required. Let me give an example. In a very ordinary case, say in the magistrates' court, one witness might say that

he went to the races by car. Another witness is called who says that he
and the previous witness went by bus. The unskilful advocate may well
cross-examine the witness on these lines:

Q   You say, do you, that you travelled by public transport?
Q   Do you realise that the previous witness has just said that you went
      by car, what do you say to that?
[And the witness who, if he had not already realised by the first question
that he had made a mistake, would easily be able to backtrack.]
A   Oh, I'm terribly sorry, I remember now, I had thought that my car
      was in dock that day, but now I remember, we did go by car.

The skilled advocate, on the other hand, with the forged will model in
mind, would ask questions on these lines:

Q   What number bus did you take?
Q   Did you travel upstairs or downstairs?
Q   Was there a conductor or conductress?
Q   Black or white, do you remember?

Such questions leave no opportunity of escape to the witness. You will
also find that this type of examination is very useful when two witnesses
give the same general account, but will differ widely when asked for the
kind of detail which they would only know if they were truthful. You will
have noticed that these are probing questions.

   This completes the review of the tools of cross-examination; now we
shall deal with the way in which you should prepare cross-examination.
As you will see from the examples already given, and from those to come,
these different types of question should be used in combination. For
instance, you may often begin an examination with probing questions,
with the intention of eliciting answers that you can eventually use in
confrontation.

   When you are inexperienced in cross-examination you may find it
difficult to know what to cross-examine about, save in the most obvious
cases. You will know that you have to put your case, but how it should
be done is a puzzle. In the Chancery Lane illustration you might be
tempted to put your case by simply saying 'I suggest that you did not see
my client on Saturday, but saw him on Friday at about two o'clock?' The
reply might be 'you can suggest what you like but you are wrong.' With
such a question you will have done your duty in putting your case, but

you will only have reinforced the witness's evidence. So the question is how a cross-examination, such as that illustrated, evolves.

When the examiner prepares his cross-examination he already knows exactly what he has to prove or disprove to establish his case. He also knows what the effect will be of each witness who is called against him. In the Chancery Lane example it might be that the witness who identifies the defendant as being in Ede's on the Saturday is one of a number of witnesses who purports to have seen the defendant in London on Saturday; and it is the objective of the examiner to cast doubt on the evidence of each witness. Suppose that the examiner does not have any of the massive evidence that he had in the earlier example. All he has is the account of the defendant that he was in Ede's on the Friday, and that it was raining hard all afternoon and that Saturday was sunny all day. He would base his cross-examination on the argument that if the witness can be induced to say that it was raining when he saw the defendant he will have effectively discredited his evidence. Having identified the topic which is going to be explored, the argument of the questions will be thought out. If it was raining heavily the defendant may well have been wearing a raincoat. His hair is likely to have been wet. He may have been running to keep out of the rain. He may have been taking shelter under the scaffolding lower down Chancery Lane. He may have had an umbrella, and so on; you will thus have explored the likely circumstantial details of being out in the rain. The defendant will then be asked questions in conference to elicit which of the various circumstances were relevant to that occasion. You will thus have turned the bald statement that it was raining into a detailed circumstantial account, and thereby provided yourself with the ammunition for cross-examining the witness. The next task is to think out the order in which you are going to put your questions. There are difficulties to be encountered. If you ask straight out 'was it raining' you will risk the dishonest witness flatly denying it, or at the very least realising at once the direction of your questions. Let us suppose that you have every reason to think that the witness is dishonest and will try to stick to the story that he saw the defendant on Saturday. There is a reasonable prospect that the witness will stick rigidly to the main lines of his story but will not have thought out the details. It is very unlikely that he will have gone to the trouble of finding out what the weather was like on the Saturday. When therefore you question him on the weather he will be driven to invention. It is likely that he will substitute Friday's weather for Saturday's because he will have a true recollection of the defendant in the rain on Friday. Your line of questioning may be as follows:

Q Where was the defendant when you first saw him.

Q How close to him were you?

Q How long was he in your sight altogether?

Q Did you get as close as three feet from him?

Q You would agree that you had a close view of him for upwards of two minutes?

Q Were you standing under the scaffolding to shelter from the rain?

Q Is that when you were three feet from the defendant?

Q What was he wearing?

Q Was he wearing a hat?

Q What sort of hat?

Q Did it appear to be a waterproof hat?

Q Was he wearing a raincoat?

Q Did you notice his waterproof leggings?

Q There was torrential rain at the time, wasn't there?

Q Did you get very wet too?

You will see that this line of questioning gently leads the witness into the trap that you have laid. The unsuspecting witness could be forgiven for thinking that you were playing into his hands by enabling him to give a detailed description of the defendant's clothing which he had observed from close quarters. If, however he says that he cannot remember what he was wearing you can cast considerable doubt on his powers of observation. In this type of questioning it is essential to keep the questions very short, and they should be asked as rapidly as possible. That is because you need to keep the witness under the greatest possible pressure, thus making it very difficult to fabricate answers. He will have no time to think of the consequences of his answers and he will be driven to giving a truthful account from his recollection. But suppose he gibs at last from admitting that it was raining. You then have a riposte thrown up by the answers he has already given. 'If it was not raining, did you not think it odd that he was sheltering under the scaffolding, wearing a waterproof hat, and leggings and a raincoat?'

This illustration is simple, though typical of the kind of problem with which you will be confronted every day in the courts, and particularly the criminal courts. Let me now give a more complex illustration taken from an actual case.

A young man with a shock of blond hair, and thus easily identifiable, was charged with breaking a shopwindow in a street in a seaside town. The only evidence against him was that of an off-duty police officer. His evidence was that on a Sunday morning at about 8 o'clock, he heard a lot of shouting outside his house. On looking out of his window he could see the defendant at the head of a group of youths who were making their way down the road towards the shop, the window of which was broken a few minutes later. The officer said that he had immediately realised that the youths were likely to be up to some sort of mischief, and he had gone to see what was happening. On going out he was in time to see the defendant throw a brick through the shop window.

The defence to this allegation was a denial that it was he who broke the window, but an admission that he was there, and an admission that he was at the front of the group at the time when he passed the policeman's house.

The starting point in preparation was to accept that the defendant was truthful in his denial of the charge, but there was no other information available. One way of getting more information for use in cross-examination in a variety of cases, both criminal and civil, is to visit the scene of the incident and see for yourself the lie of the land. In this case the policeman's house gave onto a narrow lane. About 80 yards down the lane was the shop where the window had been broken. If you stood in the doorway of the policeman's house it was not possible to see any part of the window which had been broken, because a slight bend in the lane obscured the view. Only if you crossed the lane and stood on the far side from the policeman's house could you obtain a clear view of the window which had been broken. The argument which was founded on this observation was that the officer could only have seen the breaking of the window if he had come out of his house and crossed the lane or gone down towards the shop. In the statement which he had made he said nothing about crossing the lane or specifically taking up a position from which he could see that window. That was odd, because you might have expected a witness to say how he had got into a position to see what had happened. The next stage of the preparation for cross-examination was to scrutinise all the known facts and to see whether a hypothesis could be constructed which accommodated all of them. The salient facts were that it was a Sunday morning at about 8 o'clock. The witness was a policeman. He had undoubtedly recognised the defendant correctly as being at the front of the group when they passed his house; the defendant's shock of hair was easily recognisable and in any event he admitted it. The window could not be seen from the doorstep of the policeman's house. The defendant was adamant that he had not broken the window.

An hypothesis or argument which met all these facts was as follows. The policeman might have been on a late shift on Saturday night, and was still asleep at 8 o'clock in the morning. The probability was that he had Sunday morning off and he was making the best of it. If he had been disturbed by the shouting he was probably annoyed at being woken up. He may have jumped out of bed and hurried to the window to see what was happening. What he saw made him think that this crowd of youths were on the rampage and he thought he might as well try to see if they did any mischief. He rushed downstairs because his view from upstairs was so restricted. He opened the front door and then realised that he was still in his pyjamas. He paused and felt too embarrassed to go out in his pyjamas in front of that crowd of ribald hooligans. He then heard the window break. As he had seen the defendant a minute or two before at the front of the crowd, and being unscrupulous, he allowed himself to allege that the defendant had done it.

It may be helpful, at this stage of the analysis, to take stock of the difficulties which confronted the examiner in deciding how to question the witness. The first and most obvious problem is that the hypothesis might be wrong, and then it is important to be able to withdraw from that line of questioning and pursue another. If the hypothesis is wrong it means that the witness was in a position to see the window broken, and it will be more difficult to show that he did not see what happened; yet, for example, his view might have been obscured by the group of people. The argument then would be to show that the witness was some distance behind the group and that he could easily be mistaken as to who broke the window. While this line of examination is far less likely to be decisive, it is an effective second line of attack, and should be kept in readiness should it be needed.

The next question to consider is how to structure the examination so as to give it the best prospect of success. If, for example, the examiner were to rush boldly in, the examination would almost certainly fail. The witness, were he to be asked the crucial question 'Where were you standing when you saw the window broken', would very likely say 'Just outside my house, I had a very good view.' It is necessary to approach the crucial questions by an indirect route; to force the witness along in such a way that before he realizes what is happening, he has committed himself to a position from which he cannot withdraw. In addition the examiner will be hoping to disguise the direction of his questions from the witness, and indeed from the tribunal, in the early stages, because if he finds that the hypothesis is showing signs of being wrong, he can withdraw without causing any damage to his case.

The early stages of the examination must be designed to test the accuracy of the hypothesis. For example:

Q   Were you on duty on Saturday?
Q   At what time did you finish your tour of duty?
Q   When were you to be on duty again?
Q   What time did you get home on Saturday night/Sunday morning?
Q   I expect you went straight to bed?
Q   No doubt you were looking forward to a lie-in?
Q   And as it turned out you were woken by hooligans outside?

It will be seen that these questions are framed precisely along the lines of the argument which forms the hypothesis. Once the examiner has established the late night and the morning off-duty, he knows that he is on the right track and he begins to jostle the witness along by insinuating questions. The reason for this is that the answers to these questions are known and at this stage of the questioning the examiner is winning the confidence of the witness. It will seem to the witness that the questions are entirely harmless and in fact confirming his account of what happened. The examiner then comes to the first difficult part of the examination. What he wants the witness to say is that he jumped out of bed, still in his nightwear, and went straight to the window. It is crucial that he establishes that he was in his nightwear at this early stage in such a way that the witness does not appreciate its significance. For example:

Q   Were you cross?
[This question is to distract the mind of the witness. It does not matter at all what the answer is, but the witness is likely to think that it is a hostile question and will wonder for a moment or two what its drift is.]
Q   Well cross enough to jump out of bed and go to the window?
Q   Still in your pyjamas?
Q   And you saw the group of rowdies?
Q   About how many were there?
Q   Certainly more than a dozen?
Q   Were they spread out or tightly bunched?
Q   Were they all, or some of them, similarly dressed?
Q   And of similar age?
Q   And height?

These last six questions are designed to provide the examiner with material if he has to use his second line of attack. The argument would then be that the witness could be mistaken as to who broke the window.

The questions also serve the secondary purpose of keeping the witness completely unaware of the real line of attack. The next crucial point which should, if possible, be established is the time which elapsed between the witness seeing the group and the window being broken. The examiner wants that time to be as short as possible so that it will be very difficult for the witness to say that he had time to pull on his clothes. This is an example of foreseeing an escape route and blocking it.

Q   You saw the defendant at the head of this group?
Q   It was his hair which made him stand out?
Q   Were they running or walking?
Q   How long did it take for the group to pass your window?
Q   They were moving fast weren't they?
Q   You agree that it was no more than a few seconds?
Q   And they were going to your left?
Q   Did you think they were up to no good?
Q   Was it their mood which made you think it?
Q   You, a policeman, must have been anxious to see what they were up to?
Q   How far down the lane is the shop where the window was broken?
Q   You say no more than 70 to 80 yards?

The examiner has now established that if the witness says that he saw what happened he must have got himself downstairs immediately, and he has thus created the necessary answer to any attempt by the witness to say that he dressed before going downstairs. Having thus secured his position he could continue with strongly insinuating questions.

Q   I suppose you rushed down stairs?
Q   Did you open the front door?

The examiner has now reached the vital point in the examination, and he has reached it without the witness having grasped its drift. Everyone except the examiner has probably forgotten for the moment that the witness is now at the front door in his pyjamas. The next few questions need to be asked rapidly to keep the witness under strong pressure, leaving him no time to think.

Q   You were still in your pyjamas?
Q   There were more than a dozen hooligans?
Q   If they were to see you in your pyjamas you thought they might turn on you?

Q   You stayed inside your front door didn't you?
Q   And were there when you heard the glass break?

If the witness had been quick-witted enough and brazen enough to pretend that he had gone out in his pyjamas, the examiner was ready to deal with it.

Q   Are you really saying that you risked going outside in your pyjamas.
Q   You had no shoes on?
Q   The lane is covered in grit?
Q   They might well have turned on you?
Q   They would certainly have ridiculed you?
Q   You did not go outside did you?
Q   Where do you say you were when the shop window was broken?

A dishonest witness, to cope with these questions, is likely to try to limit the extent to which he ventured out, and the questions are designed to tempt him to say that he remained close to the house so that he could dart back in. The examiner is still holding in reserve his final question by way of confrontation.

Q   You know perfectly well that you can only see the window that was broken if you stand on the other side of the lane from your doorway?
Q   You could not have seen the person who broke the window.

In the event the witness, when confronted with the fact that he could not see the window from his doorway, admitted that he had not seen the window broken; and the case was stopped immediately.

There are a number of things to be noted in this examination which may give guidance in different situations which may arise.

Forming an hypothesis is a useful device which can be used in almost every type of examination. Its advantage is that it gives you the clearest idea of what facts you must establish with the witness; you know what is relevant and irrelevant, and you know when to stop.

There are rules which you should follow when creating a hypothesis. It must always be based on all the facts of the case. If it is not so founded, it is likely to be wrong, and in any event is likely to be unethical. In the illustration the hypothesis was firmly based on the defendant's instructions; he was there but he did not do it. The imaginative part of the hypothesis was to accommodate all the facts available to explain what really happened, consistent with the instructions given by the defendant. You must not in any circumstances invent a defence by going outside your instructions.

The construction of hypotheses almost always requires an analysis of the facts of the case. In making that analysis you should form the habit of looking out for the unlikely detail, the odd fact, inconsistencies of fact or conduct, peculiar remarks or use of words by witnesses. In short, anything out of the ordinary should be noted and considered. You will find that it is very often the small detail which will give a basis for your hypothesis. One or two illustrations may be useful. I recall a social occasion when the topic of conversation was adoption. Our hostess said that she thought the optimum age for adoption was seven. A doctor in the company asked her what had happened to her when she was seven. (The answer was that her parents had separated.) That is an obvious example of an odd remark which on enquiry throws up an explanation which could have been guessed.

Here is another example, taken from an actual case. The defendant was charged with conspiracy to forge post office books. There was no direct evidence against him. His alleged co-conspirators had implicated him. He was interviewed by the police. The following is an extract from the interview.

Q [Policeman] This whole matter requires a detailed investigation and I am telling you that if you are in any way implicated it is right that at this stage and time you should be given an opportunity of saying your side of the story.

A [Defendant] Look, I will level with you. I have never passed any false Giro cheques and I'm surprised that my son-in-law is involved and that he has got my boy involved, but I'll tell you this, H has been on about Giro cheques to me for months and months. He knows I know a little about the print game and he has been asking me what is possible. I gave him advice on how he could go about it, nothing more.

Q Did you receive any money for this advice?

A No, that was months ago. I didn't think that he would have the bottle to go through with it, but he told me that if he ever came up trumps with it I would get a hundred pounds. Last week he gave me twenty five pounds and he said that if this got going right he would give me another seventy five.

Q What did you think he was talking about?

A Well I assumed he was on about bent giros and that he was going to make three or four hundred out of it, but it never crossed my mind that he was going in that big. I'll tell you quite honestly, I only gave him advice because he pestered me and to get him off my back. If I had known for one moment what he was thinking of doing I would have kicked him out of the door. I wish I had, you can see now what he has done to my family.

Q I intend to charge you with conspiracy.

A If that's the case I've got nothing more to say to you.

When the officer was cross-examined for the defendant the whole of the interview quoted was denied from the words 'I'll tell you this'.

The issue was complicated by the fact that the officer who had conducted the interview was under suspension and was not called by the prosecution; and his colleague, who gave the evidence, was alleged by the defence to have been out of the room during this crucial conversation.

The task for prosecuting counsel was difficult if he was to show from this disputed conversation that the defendant had in fact been making a confession to a limited involvement in the conspiracy. The prosecution hypothesis was that this defendant was the brains behind the whole conspiracy, and when he was confronted with the statements of the co-accused he decided to try to limit his participation in the hope of being regarded as being at most on the fringes of the conspiracy. On reviewing the evidence there was one remark which was inconsistent with the account which the defendant had given and which had been specifically admitted — 'Look I'll level with you'. This is how the cross-examiner questioned the defendant:

Q Later on in the conversation did you say to the police officer 'Look I will level with you'?

A No, I did not say that.

Q 'I have never passed any forged Giro cheques. I am surprised that my son-in-law is involved and that he has got my boy involved'?

A I said something like that, yes.

Q Did you say 'Look, I will level with you'?

A No, I am sure I did not.

Q You are sure you did not?

A I am sure.

Q Are you making that up now?

A Certainly not. There is no reason to make it up. It is not a damaging phrase, I do not think.

Q It is not a damaging phrase?

A No, but I did not say 'Look, I will level with you'.

Notes.

(1)   With the first question the examiner has extracted a denial of what counsel for the defence had actually conceded. The witness, who was very astute, realised as soon as the question was put, that it was a damning expression to have used.

(2)   The fourth question echoes the answer so as to underline it and make the witness as uncomfortable as possible. The fifth question maintains the pressure, and drives the witness into a revealing concession: 'It is not a damaging phrase'. The examination continued:

Q   What does it mean to your way of thinking?
A   Look, I will tell you.
Q   Tell you what?
A   Whatever may be coming next, depending on what you are speaking about at the time, you say 'Look, I will level with you'.
Q   What could it mean in that sense?
A   It depends on how you want to interpret it. I do not know.
Q   Well tell me
A   Look, I will tell you. To me it means look I will tell you.
Q   Tell you what though?
A   Well it may be what you are discussing about at the time. If you are talking about horses, you will say 'Look I will level with you about the horses or cats and dogs or anything else'.
Q   That is the way you interpret it?
A   That is the way I interpret it.
Q   You remember that the officer said that he understood it to mean 'I will tell you the truth'?
A   That may be the officer's interpretation of it because of his job.
Q   Do you think that that is a wrong interpretation to put on it?
A   I think it is neither wrong nor right. It depends on how you want to interpret it. I am not very well-equipped to have verbal battles with anybody.
Q   You see, you appreciate now, that if it does mean that 'I will tell the truth', it is a very damaging remark, isn't it?
A   I have no idea.
Q   You have no idea?
A   It depends on how you interpret it. I do not interpret it any other way than I have said. You may interpret it as you wish.
Q   You see the point don't you?
A   I see the point you are trying to make certainly.

Q You do?

A I would be a fool not to.

Q What point am I trying to make?

A You are trying to get me to say 'Look I will level with you' saying 'Now I will tell you the truth', or something like that. I think it is quite apparent to everybody in the court surely.

Q Indicating that up to then you had not been telling the truth?

A I did not. It may indicate it to you but I hope it does not indicate it to the jury.

Q You appreciate that when your learned counsel was cross-examining the police officer that particular phrase was not challenged and was in fact conceded?

A I do not remember.

Q Try and remember

A It is no good me trying to remember. When I say I do not remember I mean I do not remember.

Q You are now denying that you said it because you realise the importance of the remark, isn't that right?

A That is not true at all.

Q You began that part of the interview by telling the police officers that you were going to tell the truth?

A What, that part 'Look I will level with you'?

Q Didn't you?

A No, I did not.

Q Then you went on to describe your part in this affair, didn't you?

A It would have been a very foolish thing to do, but I did not do it.

Q You were trying to minimise the part that you were playing in it?

A I did not have to try to minimise it, because I did not have any part in it.

Notes.

   (1)   The meaning of the phrase is perfectly obvious, but the examiner resourcefully capitalises on the witness' denial that it was a damaging phrase. 'What does it mean to your way of thinking' is very skilfully put. It prevents this clever and elusive witness from hiding behind the 'It could mean what you choose' type of answer. The witness is forced into committing himself to a positive answer. In the next few questions the examiner forces him to elaborate on that initial commitment, while all the time the jury are contrasting his answers with the obvious meaning of the phrase. These probing questions bring the witness under such pressure that his replies become absurd.

(2)   Quoting the officer's evidence as to what the phrase meant is very neat; it puts in the mouth of the officer what everybody is thinking; it parries the witness' skilful attempt to involve the examiner in a personal argument and it contrasts the obvious with the absurd.

(3)   The probing questions which follow prod the witness until he is forced by the atmosphere in court to concede the force of the argument. He is then confronted with the concession made by his own counsel.

(4)   The examiner is never deflected from his objective, and keeps the witness under relentless pressure.

(5)   The witness was evidently taken by surprise when the phrase was attacked. The element of surprise is a formidable weapon, and as we shall see later on, can often be used to great effect at the beginning of a cross-examination. Here the attack was made well into the cross-examination, primarily to avoid the possibility of the witness recovering from its effect. You may wonder how the examiner could be so confident that his examination would be successful on this phrase. The answer lies in the hypothesis. The witness wanted to minimise his part in the conspiracy when he realised how much the police knew. As he wanted to accept that he had said to the police 'I have never passed any forged Giro cheques and I am surprised that my son-in-law is involved and that he has got my boy involved', it was evident that he had actually used those words in interview. Those words had been preceded by 'I will level with you', which his counsel had accepted had been used. If they had not been used the defendant himself would have been very anxious to deny them. He would have said to his counsel 'Look how they are trying to frame me by putting in that phrase with all it implies'. So the examiner was as certain as could be that those words had in fact been used by the defendant. That meant that when asked about them, conscious as he was of what he had said and why he had said it, he would be under immense pressure once he realised that he had overlooked their significance. He was in the impossible position of having conceded that they were used. He had no way out; and so it did not matter what he answered so long as the examination was conducted with requisite skill. The only point which had to be made was that the defendant at that part of the interview was saying that he was about to tell the truth, when before he had not, and that in using that phrase he must have been referring to the limited involvement he was confessing and not merely to his denial of passing forged cheques and his surprise that his son-in-law was involved.

You will see from this analysis that the preparation of the cross-examination requires careful thought about what actually happened in any given situation. This always needs an evaluation of the probabilities. It is also necessary to cultivate the habit of noticing how types of people behave. In court you can often identify a type, which is a preliminary guide to the particular way in which he might behave in a given situation. To take a simple example, a courageous type would show defiance in the face of threats, where as the pusillanimous would be on the retreat. When you have identified the type, listen carefully to what is said, and always note when you would have expected something to be said, and it is not. In the plate-glass window case you would have expected the witness to have said that he crossed the road if he had done so, and his failure to mention it increased the probability that he had not. It is very difficult for an untruthful person to conceal for long under examination the fact that he is concealing something: he will inevitably give himself away by the words he uses, particularly when he is questioned on matter which he has not prepared. Look again at some of the answers given by the witness who was not prepared to level with the court. For example, one of the first things he said was that it 'was not a damaging phrase'. He had in fact just realised that that was exactly what it was, and it bubbled out in spite of himself.

One of the reasons why the formulation of a hypothesis is so useful is because no event occurs in isolation. All events take place in connection with, or in relation to, other events. Any account given by a witness of an event must necessarily be associated with a whole train of events. If what the witness says is true it must fit in exactly with every other event with which it is connected, down to the minutest detail. And yet, on the other hand, if the story is untrue there will be many points in the surrounding circumstances where the story told will not fit. The way then to expose what is untrue is to examine the detail of the surrounding circumstances. The shopwindow case is a vivid illustration. The formulation of a hypothesis enables the examiner to see in a plain way the whole of the transaction including its circumstantial detail, so that he can explore with surgical accuracy every aspect of the transaction down to the smallest detail. He always has in his mind what in all probability actually happened to compare with what the witness is saying happened.

A common error in cross-examination is to ask questions about an aspect of the witness' evidence, the circumstantial detail of which the cross-examiner knows little or nothing. The witness can therefore make replies which it is impossible to check against known or probable facts. The hypothesis is a useful guide to the focus of the cross-examination and should prevent you from straying outside it. The maxim is never to ask a question to which you have no riposte; that is a very different thing from the inappropriate maxim 'Never ask a question to which you do not know the answer'. If that maxim were adhered to, many questions which ought to be asked would not be asked, and perhaps a winning point would be lost.

The order in which you ask questions and the structure of your cross-examination as a whole, should be carefully thought out. In an ordinary cross-examination you will be able, after a little practice, to think out the order on the spot; but in a complex case, it may be necessary to prepare very carefully the design of your examination. As has already been said the fundamental rule is to examine along the lines of the argument. It may be useful at this stage to look at some of the problems which may arise in preparing your cross-examination and to consider possible solutions.

Your first consideration should be to consider whether it is necessary to cross-examine at all. In this respect you will bear in mind that you will have to put your case as previously discussed; and you will also consider whether there is any aspect of the evidence given by the witness which should in any way be clarified, amplified or undermined. Always avoid unnecessary cross-examination.

Two illustrations may be given. The first was a case where the accused was charged with obtaining property by deception. The defendant was a black woman with a very conspicuous limp. The case against her was that she had obtained a fur coat by deception. It was said that she had gone into a fur shop; she had chosen a coat; she paid for it with a cheque drawn on her own bank account which was in funds and said that she would collect the coat later during the week. The same day she countermanded the cheque. She said the reason for doing so was that she had decided she did not want the coat after all. None of this was disputed by the defendant. Her defence was that when she had decided not to have the coat, and once she had countermanded the cheque she had nothing more to do with the transaction, until she was interviewed by the police.

But the prosecution said that after countermanding the cheque she had gone back to the shop after a few days, and that she had been given the coat by the manager of the shop who had recognised her as soon as she came in. When her home was searched there was no sign of the coat. The sole evidence against her, therefore, was the identification of her by the shop manager. The defence was that he had made a mistake in thinking that it was the defendant who had returned to the shop and collected the coat.

Prosecuting counsel examined in chief by eliciting from the shop manager that it was the defendant who had chosen the coat and presented the cheque on the first occasion. That was, of course admitted. He made the mistake, however, of failing to ask the witness to describe the person who had come into the shop on the first occasion. The witness was then asked what happened a few days later and he said that the same woman had come into the shop. He had recognised her at once, and had handed her the coat and she had left with it. Again, and this was a more serious error, the witness was not asked to describe the person who had collected the coat.

These were the circumstances in which defence counsel had to consider how to cross-examine. He was obliged to put his case, which was that the witness had made a mistake in thinking that the woman who collected the coat was the same person who had presented the cheque on the first occasion. The danger of any prolonged cross-examination was that at any moment, if the witness was right, something said might spark a recollection that the woman on both occasions had a pronounced limp. Likewise, if he was a dishonest witness he might remember that the woman on the first occasion had a limp and bolster his identification by saying that the woman to whom he gave the coat had a similar limp, whether she did or not. It was necessary, therefore, to confine the cross-examination to one question: 'You made a mistake in thinking that the woman who collected the coat was the same person who presented the cheque?' It sounded like a preliminary question and got the reply, 'I don't think I was mistaken'. The form of the question had to be carefully thought out so as to run the least risk of provoking the witness into searching his recollection for the reason why he said that it was the defendant on both occasions. It was likewise important to avoid prompting prosecuting counsel to ask the questions in re-examination which he should have asked in chief. In the result it was possible to submit at the close of the prosecution case that the evidence of identity was too slender to found a conviction. There had been no identification parade and there was a real probability that the witness was mistaken. It was only in the course of submissions that prosecuting counsel was informed by the police officer in charge of the case that the defendant had a limp. It was then too late to admit it in evidence and the defendant was acquitted.

You will notice from this case that defence counsel had thought out exactly what he needed to found his defence and at the same time to put his case to the witness, and he strongly resisted the temptation to expand his examination in any way.

The second example illustrates what can happen when an unnecessary question is asked. A man was charged with stealing lead from the roof of a derelict house. The only evidence against him was that of a police officer who said that he saw the defendant in the garden of the house and that he had lead dust on his hands. The defence was that the defendant had gone to the house because he had been told that there was work there. When he arrived he could find nobody and he had just climbed into the house to see if anybody was about. In doing so he had got house dust on his hands. It was clearly necessary for defence counsel to put to the policeman that he was mistaken in saying that the defendant had lead dust on his hands. Having put that question he went further:

Q   You realise that if the defendant climbed into the house, he would have got house dust on his hands?
A   Yes, very probably.
Q   Are you seriously saying that you can tell the difference between house dust and lead dust?
A   Well, as a matter of fact I think I can. Before I joined the police, I worked for British Rail, and often worked with lead there.

The last question was wholly unnecessary. It could have been left for comment: 'Do you think, members of the jury, the constable could have told the difference between house dust and lead dust without examining the defendant's hands minutely?

Even though a very damaging answer had been elicited by the unnecessary question a skilful examiner could have rescued the situation. In the event the Judge did it for him:

Q   Where was the lead you worked with at British Rail?
A   Beside the track.
Q   Was all the lead you worked with beside the track?
A   Yes.
Q   That lead is invariably covered in grease isn't it?
A   Yes.

It is worth noting that this examination typifies the way in which a witness should be tied down to a specific fact, namely that he only worked with lead that was beside the track. Had that not been established the witness, if dishonest, could have escaped by saying that he did work with lead which was not greasy and which gave off a residue of dust.

If you have decided that it is necessary to cross-examine you must then decide how you will begin. This decision inevitably depends on a multitude of circumstances, but it may be useful to discuss some of the considerations which may influence you in your decision. Suppose that you want to shake the confidence of an untruthful witness or of one who pretends to be what he is not. A surprise question right at the outset is likely to damage the witness in the eyes of the tribunal, and make it difficult for the witness to recover his composure. A number of examples can be given. Rufus Isaacs' second question in the *Seddon* case (*Notable English Trials*, p. 170) is justly regarded as a classic. Seddon was accused of murdering an elderly woman who had lodged with him and his wife. She was, by common consent, somewhat eccentric and was apparently more or less friendless. On any view Seddon had treated her meanly while she lodged in his house.

Q   Miss Barrow lived with you from 26 July 1910 till the morning of 14 September 1911?
A   Yes.
Q   Did you like her?
A   Did I like her?
Q   Yes, that is the question.
A   She was not a woman you could be in love with, but I deeply sympathised with her.

Another classic question was that of Norman Birkett in the *Rouse* case (Bowker, *Behind the Bar*, p. 216). Part of the evidence in the trial for murder concerned the remains of a burnt-out car. An 'expert' was called by the defence and he drew very confident conclusions from the remains of the vehicle. A brass nut on the petrol pipe was found to be loose after the fire, and the prosecution alleged that proved the fire was non-accidental. The witness describing himself as an engineer and assessor said that the fire was accidental and that the nut could have come loose in the fire. Birkett's cross-examination began:

Q   What is the co-efficient of the expansion of brass?
A   I'm afraid I cannot answer the question off-hand.
Q   If you do not know, say so. What do I mean by the term?
A   You want to know what is the expansion of the metal under heat?
Q   I asked you what is the co-efficient of the expansion of brass. Do you know what it means?
A   Put that way, probably I do not.
Q   You are an engineer?
A   I dare say I am.

Q Well you are not a doctor, or a crime investigator or an amateur detective are you?

A No.

Q Are you an engineer?

A Yes.

Q What is the co-efficient of the expansion of brass? Do you know?

A No, not put that way.

[This passage is cited in *The Art of the Advocate*, Richard Du Cann, p. 114, Pelican; and a slightly different version in Montgomery Hyde's *Life of Birkett*, Penguin, 1964, p. 307.]

Notes.

(1)   It is evident that Birkett had a shrewd idea that this witness was either unknown as an engineer, or more likely known as a charlatan. He therefore hit on a question which a genuine engineer would probably be able to answer in a comprehensible way. The follow-up question is very skilful. While being absolutely fair, it brings great pressure on the witness. If he says that he does not know, he is admitting his ignorance and so he is virtually forced into attempting an explanation. Asked many years later what he would have done if the witness had given the correct answer, he said that he would have gone on to copper, then to aluminium and other metals, eventually leaving the subject as if it were of no particular importance. (See Montgomery Hyde, *loc. cit.* p. 309.)

(2)   The following questions harping on his being an engineer and not anything else, are well contrasted with his inability to answer the technical question.

Turning to another example, a man was charged with stealing a valuable ring from his employers' jewellery shop. His defence was that he had borrowed it overnight. In the course of his evidence in chief he had said that he had told his mother that it was an engagement ring for his girlfriend. The first question in cross-examination was 'Why did you lie to your mother'.

In another case where the defendant was charged with fraud, it was relevant to his defence to make out that he was a Doctor of Divinity. It was evident that he was an uneducated man. The first two questions were 'What is the Pentateuch?' 'Do you think you can eat it?'

The art of this type of question is to gauge accurately from known facts about the witness what his response is likely to be, and how best to take him by surprise.

Another situation which frequently arises is where the witness has given damaging evidence which needs to be attacked, but may well be able to give evidence which you require to support your case. In these circumstances it would be foolish to unsettle the witness, or to antagonise him by launching an immediate attack. The shopwindow case referred to earlier is a good example of this situation.

Sometimes you may want to give the tribunal a vignette of the witness and the case against him. A striking example is Carson's opening questions of Oscar Wilde.

Q   You stated that your age was 39. I think you are over 40. You were born on 16 October 1854?

A   I have no wish to pose as being young. I am 39 or 40. You have my certificate and that settles the matter.

Q   But being born in 1854 makes you more than 40?

A   Ah, very well.

The final example of the opening questions of a cross-examination is Sir Richard Muir's examination of Crippen. It is a perfect model of its kind.

Q   On the morning of the first of February you were left alone in your house with your wife?

A   Yes.

Q   She was alive?

A   She was.

Q   And well?

A   She was.

Q   Do you know of any person in the world who has seen her alive since?

A   I do not.

Q   Do you know of any person in the world who has ever had a letter from her since?

A   I do not.

Q   Do you know of any person in the world who can prove any fact showing that she ever left that house alive?

A   Absolutely not. I have told Mr Dew exactly all the facts.

As is usual with all the examinations we have looked at the questions are the individual steps of an argument. In this instance these few questions would probably have been sufficient to seal Crippen's fate. They are deadly because they show so simply and starkly what he must have done. We saw earlier in the extract from the trial of Dickman how the examiner questioned the witness on different topics and dealt with each topic completely before passing on to the next. Whether the examination is long or short this technique should be adopted. Careful thought should be given to the order in which the topics are to be dealt with. Your primary consideration will be to adhere to the logical sequence of your overall argument, but sometimes for tactical reasons you may want to adopt a different order for the purpose for example, of establishing facts with which you wish to confront the witness later on.

The order of your questions on each topic must also be carefully considered. Order is always important where you are trying to pin a witness down to a particular account. It is necessary to seal off any escape route for the witness. This must be done by foreseeing which way the witness will be likely to run when he realises that he is being netted.

In the following example the accused was a milk-roundsman who was charged with stealing money from his takings. His defence was that he had not stolen any money, and if any was missing it was the result of dishonesty or incompetence by his manager. The evidence showed that on the day when the defendant was alleged to have stolen the money there was a breach of the company's rules by the manager. A roundsman's paying-in slip, ought to have been made out in duplicate. One of the two slips should have been given to the defendant, but it was found in the manager's office with the top slip. In addition the slip itself, which should have been signed by the roundsman, had been signed on that occasion by the manager. Part of the cross-examination of the manager was as follows:

Q Who makes out the paying-in slips?
A The roundsman himself.
Q Does he write it out?
A Yes.
Q The whole of it?
A Yes.
Q And sign it?
A Yes.
Q Are there any circumstances in which you would do that?
A No, but can I say that I think there was one occasion where a chap cut his hand falling over with glass; we counted the money together and he asked me to sign it.
Q Unless there is an emergency the roundsman fills in the whole of the document and signs it?

A Yes, unless there is an extreme emergency.

Q And would it be right to say that it would be quite unusual for the company to keep both the top copy of the paying-in slip and the carbon copy which is normally retained by the roundsman?

A Yes.

Q Wholly exceptional?

A Yes.

Q On Saturday, 6 July there was no emergency of any kind was there?

A I cannot remember any, I cannot remember any at all.

Q If there had been it would be something which would stick out in your memory, wouldn't it?

A Well, there was nothing unusual that I remember.

Q Please will you look at this exhibit. It is the roundsman's slip for 6 July?

A Yes, that is correct.

Q The next slip is the carbon copy?

A Yes.

Q Whose writing is that?

A It is definitely my writing.

Q Is the whole of it, including the signature, in your writing?

A Yes, I would say it was.

Q You know your own writing, is it yours or not?

A Yes, it is.

Q Why did you sign his document?

A Well I can only say that on this particular evening he must have been very, very late, in which case I do what I can to help them to get home. Their families worry and we get wives ringing up asking where they are. Possibly I signed his slip for him while he was counting the money.

Q You are saying that you filled in that slip and signed it in order to help him?

A Yes.

Q Do you remember doing that?

A I often do that.

Q Often?

A Not often, well if a man is late. As I have said before. If a man is late or is injured in some way I would do it to help him.

Q Why did you sign his name to look like a signature?

A Well I just asked him, do you want me to sign it? In whose name?

Q You have spelt his name wrong haven't you?

A I thought that was the way.
Q It is not normal practice to sign the roundsman's slip?
A No.
Q That is because it is a form of check for the roundsman?
A Yes.
Q His only form of check?
A Yes.
Q It is therefore a matter of importance to you, signing his document, to make sure that he is given his copy?
A It would be, yes.
Q Why then didn't you make sure that he had the carbon copy?
A I would have. I would have handed it to him at the time.
Q You signed that document in his absence didn't you?
A No.
Q That is why he never got his copy?
A I can't say.

Note.
The order in which the questions are asked is all important. The witness is tied down to a particular account. All escape routes are blocked off, and then he is confronted with the document which gives the lie to what he has said.

(1)   The argument which informs this examination is that the witness had the opportunity to take or carelessly lose the money which was missing. There was a safeguard to protect the roundsman from accusations of theft in the system laid down. The roundsman should have been supervised and enabled to sign his own document and to have retained the carbon copy of it. It was the manager's duty to see that the rules were observed, but the fact was that he had breached them himself.

(2)   The opening questions are probing and designed to compel the witness to admit that it was only in exceptional circumstances that the manager would sign the slip. You will notice that the examiner holds back his strong point, that the filling in and signing and retention of the carbon copy was the only safeguard which the roundsman had. The reason for not using this point earlier in the examination was to have it in reserve to meet any suggestion that it was perfectly all right for the manager to sign for the roundsman. You can see how it was used later on to enforce the carbon copy point. Notice particularly that the examiner is not content with the answer to the general question 'who makes out the paying in

slips', but obtains an answer to each detail of the making out of the slips. This is a very important technique because it makes it difficult for the witness to invent a way out; the exactness of the questions keeps him under pressure.

(3)   When it has been firmly established that the manager would only sign in an extreme emergency, the examiner then moves on to the absence of any emergency on the day in question. It is obvious that if he had dealt with these two points in the reverse order he would have run the risk of a cunning witness making out that there were numerous situations where the rules were breached in order to help the roundsman. As it is, the witness tried that tack, but he was already enmeshed in the questions by the time he realised he was in danger. You will notice that the examiner has employed insinuating questions to compel the witness to agree that there was no emergency.

(4)   The examiner does not allow the witness to get away with any vagueness in his answers about the writing on the slip.

(5)   Not much is made of the point that the writing of the name on the slip has been made to look like a signature. Had the object been to show that the witness was undoubtedly dishonest this point would have been used to greater effect, but because it was not necessary to go so far, the point was merely used as an additional fact in the presentation of what had happened.

We shall next consider the cross-examination of the scrap-metal dealer whose examination in chief was criticised in Chapter Three. Mr Z was first asked about misrepresenting the number of shares he had owned in the company. The jury were thus immediately presented with a man who for some inexplicable reason was telling a lie. As soon as the point had been made the examiner then passed to the next topic:

Q   You heard your employee, Mr H. say in evidence that your company has nothing to do with Blogg's company. Was that true?

A   Yes.

Q   Do you know anybody who is a director of Blogg's company?

A   My brother.

Q   What is his name?

A   Graham.

Q   Is he in any way connected with your company?

A   No, he used to be.

Q   Have you any connection with Blogg's company?

A   Who me?

Q   Yes you.
A   I lent my brother some money, yes.
Q   How much?
A   £10,000.
Q   When?
A   1978.
Q   As long ago as that was it?
A   Yes.
Q   On 30 November, 1980 didn't you lend £8,000 to Blogg's company?
A   On 30 November, 1980?
Q   Yes.
A   Yes, I did.
Q   Slipped your memory did it?
A   No, because it's been paid back.
Q   There is a close association between your company and Blogg's company isn't there?
A   No.
Q   Do you often visit Blogg's company?
A   Not often, no.

Notes.

(1)   The impression has been created that the witness is not being candid in his answers, by questions which an honest witness could be expected to answer without the slightest difficulty.

(2)   The examiner has the facts of the case and the points which he wants to use in his head; certainly at the ready. There is no question of his fumbling through his papers in order to find the fact he wants. This is an important part of the technique of examination because it contributes materially to keeping the witness under pressure. A feature of this examination is that the witness is given no time to think. The pressure he is under is reflected in his repetition of the question on one or two occasions.

The cross-examination continued on another topic: the amount of cash passing through the company, well over two million pounds. And how easy it would be to extract three to four hundred thousand pounds. The witness said that it could not have been done because of the controls. He was then asked to say precisely what the controls were. He could not do so. He was next examined on an allied topic.

Q   Did you keep a private ledger?
A   The accounts people did, yes.

Q Why?
A Why?
Q Yes, why?
A I don't know why.
Q You don't know why a private ledger was kept?
A I'm not an accountant.
Q You were running the business?
A I was one of the directors.
Q Do you mean to say that you do not know why a private ledger was kept?
A Well, I'm sorry but I don't.
Q What was put in the private ledger?
A I've never seen it.
Q What did you think it was for?
A Recording transactions.
Q What sort?
A What sort? I've no idea really, I've never given it a thought.
Q Give it a thought.
A I should say the name suggests that if any of the directors had borrowed money, or anything like that.
Q Where is the private ledger?
A I don't know, I think it's with the accountants.
[The examiner knew that the witness had no intention of producing the ledger and strongly suspected that the ledger would have shown that money was extracted from the company.]

Again these questions are asked very briskly and are designed to expose the witness as being shifty; also to point to a likely method of concealing the extraction of money.

The next topic of examination was to point to a lie he had told about his medication, and the examiner was able to confront him with the evidence of a doctor who had examined him at the police station. You will see how the topics progress from general matters to specific. Next came the only really tangible evidence against him, his remarks in interview with the police, which although not admissions were equivocal.

The final topic was to demonstrate that the witness had a motive for the conspiracy. During the period in question his company was carrying a huge overdraft.

It is worth noting that in this run of the mill examination the examiner carefully chose the particular topics on which he could make some impression, carefully arranged them in what appeared to be the most effective order and then did not allow the witness any room to evade or wriggle out of the questions. The knack is to ask very short questions which demand an answer in the terms in which they are asked. It is a skill which takes time to acquire, but will come with practice.

The concluding questions of a cross-examination, particularly of a major witness, should if possible end on a strong note. It should be the natural culmination of the argument which has been put step by step in the preceding questions.

Perhaps the most celebrated ending to a cross-examination was that of Sir Edward Carson in the Cadbury libel action in 1909. *The Evening Standard* had called the Cadburys 'a bunch of canting hypocrites', because they obtained a large part of their supply of cocoa from Sao Tome and Principe, where slave labour was used in the most horrible conditions. The final questions of the examination were:

Q From 1901 to 1908 when you ceased trading, was there anything effective you did at all?
A I think so myself. I admit that my efforts resulted in a good deal less than I would have liked, but I do not admit that I did nothing at all.
Q Have you formed any estimate of the number of slaves who lost their lives in preparing your cocoa from 1901 to 1908?
A No, no, no.

The jury found that Cadbury had been libelled, but assessed the damages at a farthing.

Although nearly all the illustrations which have been given are taken from criminal cases, you will appreciate that the principles of cross-examination which have been analysed apply equally to any type of cross-examination, and the illustrations which have been given may be used as models which can be adapted for use in a multiplicity of cases both in the civil and criminal courts.

Seven

Cross-examination of Experts

In a case of murder in which a defence of insanity was set up a medical witness gave evidence that the defendant had acted under an irresistible impulse.
Judge *Do you think that he would have acted as he did if a policeman had been present?*
Witness *No.*
Judge *Your definition of irresistible impulse, then, must be an impulse irresistible at all times except when a policeman is present.* (Best on Evidence, *12th edn.*)

There are essentially two methods of cross-examining an expert. The first is to discredit him, and the second to establish so far as is possible an alternative interpretation of the facts upon which the expert's opinion is based.

We have already seen an example of discrediting a witness by demonstrating that he was not really an expert at all (Birkett in the *Rouse* case). The opportunities of that kind of discrediting are necessarily rare. It is not infrequent, however, that a witness, although a genuine expert, has not got the facts right and therefore his conclusions will be wrong. I recall a case where a Home Office expert, in a child abuse case, gave evidence to support the prosecution entirely based on photographs of the injuries caused to the child. The defence had an expert who had examined the child and was able to say that the Home Office expert's conclusion was certainly erroneous because an actual examination disclosed a type of blister which could not have been caused in the way alleged by the prosecution.

A similar example was where an expert in a building case had not troubled to visit the site, and he had been misinformed on a crucial fact which affected the conclusions he had reached. In this type of case it is often necessary for the cross-examiner to have the benefit of his own expert's advice, although some practitioners by dint of experience become more or less experts themselves. Another method of undermining the conclusions of an expert is to show that the field of expertise is not capable of yielding certain results. That is, for example, to some extent true with handwriting experts. Such experts frequently labour under the great difficulty of having only a fragment of writing to compare with known writing, and in forgery cases, the likelihood that the unknown writing may have been disguised. The scope for cross-examination on these lines is plain and needs no further comment. The cross-examination of experts in order to place a different interpretation on established facts is probably the most difficult type of cross-examination to accomplish successfully. There are several reasons for this: it is necessary for the cross-examiner himself to have a complete working knowledge of the expert's subject as well as of the facts of the instant case; the expert is also likely to be something of a professional witness and has been cross-examined many times before so that he has his responses to the theoretical side of his expertise well thought out and rehearsed; and finally it is more than usually difficult to prevent the witness from taking advantage of a loosely framed question. It is necessary for the examiner to prepare his examination in such a way that he minimises these difficulties, and in particular he should strive to make every question as sharp and pointed as possible in order to compel the witness to answer it in the terms in which it is asked. The preparation of such an examination should be founded on the same principles already discussed, but emphasis should be given to the argument which you are advancing as the alternative interpretation of the facts. This should enable you to put your finger on the point or points of divergence between the expert you are examining and the expert who is assisting you. It is these points of divergence which must form the basis of the examination.

The cross-examination by Marshall Hall of Sir William Willcox in the trial of the Seddons has always been regarded as a fine example of the cross-examination of an expert. The theory of the prosecution, founded on Sir William's evidence, was that Miss Barrow had died of acute arsenical poisoning which meant that poison had been administered within 24 hours of death. The only people in a position to do so were the Seddons. The defence was that Miss Barrow had died from epidemic diarrhoea, possibly aggravated by 'chronic' arsenical poisoning, which meant that she had been taking arsenic over a prolonged period before death. Marshall Hall's aim was to show, if he could, that the quantity of arsenic found in the body was one consistent with chronic, as opposed to acute, poisoning. The prosecution case on this point stood or fell on the evidence of Willcox who had calculated the amount of arsenic in the body by means of an experiment which had never before been relied on in a court of law. By weighing the amount of arsenic in the liver and intestines and by using 'Marsh's test' for the rest of the body he calculated that there were 2.01 grains of arsenic in the body at the time of his examination. That was enough to constitute a fatal dose, but since arsenic is very quickly expelled from the body, he estimated that at least 5 grains of arsenic had been administered to Miss Barrow shortly before the time of death. The difficulty in the evidence was that the actual amount of arsenic in the body which it was possible to weigh, that in the liver and intestines, was only 0.63 of a grain. The remainder was calculated by a complex scientific experiment. Marshall Hall therefore examined Willcox so as to cast doubt on the accuracy of the experiment. In the following passage his purpose is to show that any initial error made in the experiment would be multiplied hundreds, and in some instances, thousands of times in the calculations which followed.

Q   You have to heat the tube?
A   The substance to be tested is really in the hydrogen apparatus.
Q   And if there is arsenic in the stuff to be tested you convert your hydrogen into arsenic salt, do you not?
A   Yes.
Q   And that deposits on the side of the heated tube in a black substance on that which you call a mirror?
A   Yes.
Q   Now the quantity of arsenic so deposited can only be estimated by comparison with known mirrors containing known quantities?
A   That is so.
Q   You first make a mirror which contains a particular quantity, and it must be very minute, because if you do not have it minute you get an opaque mirror, and you cannot see?
A   It is too big a mirror to match.
Q   Now you would agree with me as to the importance of absolute accuracy — absolute accuracy not relative accuracy?

A   It is most important to be as accurate as possible.
Q   But a very minute difference makes a very great difference in the result of arsenic calculated as in the body, does it not?
A   I fully admit that.
Q   Take for instance the lungs. The mirror that you have got shows $\frac{1}{50}$th part of a milligram, which is equivalent to $\frac{1}{3240}$th part of a grain?
A   Yes.
Q   That is what you get from a sample which weighs six grams is that not so?
A   Quite so; the multiplying factor is a big one.
Q   I daresay you will tell me the multiplying factor in order to arrive at the amount of arsenic which that particular organ contained?
A   Roughly it is 50.
Q   Therefore any error in the diagnosis of the mirror is multiplied 50 times in the calculation as to the quantity of arsenic?
A   Exactly.
Q   Would you mind telling me what the multiplying factor was in the case of the stomach?
A   The multiplying factor in the case of the stomach would be about 200. [He then went on to seek the multiplying factor in respect of each organ.]
Q   So that in every one of these cases a very minute error in the original measurement by the mirror would, of course, make a very great difference in the ultimate calculation?
A   That is so.

Notes.

(1)   The examiner demonstrates a complete command of the experiment which was carried out as well as the nature and effect of the calculations which were based on it.

(2)   He has arranged his examination so as to enable the jury to follow with perfect ease the point which he is making. He first states the point he is about to make. He then makes the point and illustrates it fully by an accumulation of instances, and rounds off the point by stating again the point he has made. The accumulation of instances is in this example most important because with each example the tribunal is likely to be weighing up the chances of error creeping into the calculations. The effect would have been much weakened if say only one instance had been given. I need hardly say that in pointing this out I have no intention of encouraging prolixity. It is matter for practical judgment to decide how much detail

to present in making a point. Here the detail is itself an intrinsic part of the argument.

   The next point to which Marshall Hall then turned was to expose the fact that Willcox had left out of account in his calculations the evaporation of water from the body after death, and in particular the evaporation of water from the muscle which in life is largely composed of water.

Q   Now in the case of the muscle, I find that the result of your calculation that in the muscle was no less than 1.03 grain of arsenic?
A   Yes.
Q   That is to say slightly more than half the total calculated weight of arsenic in the body?
A   About half.
Q   Now you have worked on the assumption that the weight of the muscle in the body is equivalent to about $^2/_5$ ths of the weight of the body. That is an accepted medical dictum is it not?
A   Yes.
Q   But this is the relative calculated weight of muscle to body in the living body is it not?
A   Yes, or in the dead body. [Immediately after death.]
Q   Now then, if you have a part of the body which in life or immediately succeeding death has a known relative proportion to the total weight of the body, the weight of the water in the whole body and of the portion, including the weight of water, both in the portion and in the whole body, will be proportionate. It must be? That is sound is it not?
A   Yes.
[The question here betrays by its obscurity a partial failure to think out precisely what he meant to express. This is particularly prone to happen when one is struggling to express the unfamiliar; as when cross-examining an expert. Here of course it was a slight and momentary lapse in an extremely skilful examination. From the comfort of the armchair you could say that the question would have been clearer if he had said 'If you have a part of the body, in life or immediately after death, with a known proportional weight to the whole, the proportional weights include the weight of water do they not?']
Q   Now in this case you have got a drying-up of the whole body all over have you?
A   Yes, some drying.
Q   The ratio of the drying is quicker in the muscle than it is in the other portions of the body?

A Not necessarily.

Q But I suggest to you that it is, the muscle contains, 77 per cent water?

A Yes.

Q According to the medical books?

A Yes.

Q Bone contains only 50 per cent, so that you see the muscle would lose water, assuming that they are all losing at the same rate, in a greater proportion; that is in the proportion of 77 to 50 over the loss in the bone?

A I agree with you as regards bone but not as regards other organs.

Q The bones dry very slowly do they not?

A They dry slowly, yes.

Q And I'm sure it was an oversight, I mean, I may be wrong, but in making this calculation you have made no allowance whatever for the loss of water?

A No I have not.

Q Do you not think you ought to have made some allowance?

A Well the calculation of muscle must only be approximate. I have estimated it as one grain. I admit that must only be approximate.

Q As far as the mirror of the muscle goes, the multiplying factor is enormous, close upon 2000, and as far as the multiple is concerned it is practically 50 per cent of the total calculation? It has a most important effect, because the result of it is to bring out 50 per cent of the total calculated arsenic in the body?

A Yes, I agree.

Note.

The examiner, having spotted the error the expert had made, exposed it by the customary step by step technique. A critical point to establish was the higher proportion of water in the muscle as opposed to the bone, because the more rapid the evaporation of water from the muscle as opposed to the bone, the greater would be the discrepancy based on the $2/5$ths proportion muscle to body. When he reached that point in the examination Willcox parried, but was forced into admission because Marshall Hall was so well prepared with the facts of water content in muscle and bone. This is a vivid example of the way in which careful preparation and planning makes all the difference between success and failure.

The final extract from this cross-examination cannot better be introduced than by a quotation from Edward Marjoribanks' *Famous Trials of Marshall Hall* (Penguin, 1950, p. 254):

Among the abundant literature which he had been perusing for the purposes of this case was the report of the Royal Commission on Arsenic, convened at the beginning of the century as a result of a widespread epidemic of arsenical poisoning arising from beer drinking. Now Marshall Hall had in the forefront of his mind every detail of the conclusions of this Commission; Sir William Willcox on the other hand, had them stored in the back of his memory, but had not read the report for some time. From a wide examination of cases the Commission had reported this: that arsenic does not penetrate even into the proximal hair (that nearest the scalp) unless taken by the person affected some weeks before, and does not penetrate to the distal hair (the hair away from the roots) unless the person affected has taken arsenic at a considerably distant period — months, perhaps years ago. For the arsenic remains in the hair as it grows, and the hair growing at about five or six inches a year, it is possible to compute how long ago the arsenic was taken by the distance it is away from the scalp of a woman with long hair. Now, Sir William Willcox had examined a portion of Miss Barrow's hair of about twelve inches in length.

The examination then went as follows (*Notable English Trials*, p. 123):

Q You are convinced, Dr Willcox, that this is a case of acute arsenical poisoning. That is your honest opinion?

A I have no doubt of it.

Q Did you examine the hair?

A Yes.

Q You did as a matter of fact examine the distal end of the hair?

A Yes I did.

Q You found in the heart $\frac{1}{160}$th of a milligram, and in the proximal end of the hair you found $\frac{1}{180}$th of a milligram?

A Yes.

Q What did you find in the distal end of the hair?

A One three thousandth, about a quarter as much.

Q You took a length of hair which was about 12 inches, I think?

A They varied. I should say the average was about 10 inches.

Q And in order that you should have a proper examination you took three inches from the distal end and three inches from the proximal end?

A Yes.

Q Was this not one of the most important subjects of investigation in the Royal Commission report on arsenic in the hair?

A Yes.

Marshall Hall then proceeded to take the witness through various passages in the report which established the facts already mentioned as having been found by the Commission. Space does not allow the passage to be quoted, but it is a good example of the way in which such a document should be used to establish points in cross examination (*loc. cit.* p. 123). He continued (p. 126):

Q   Is the finding of the arsenic in the hair corroborative of acute arsenical poisoning or of chronic arsenic taking?
A   If arsenic is found in the hair it indicates that probably the arsenic had been taken for some period.
Q   I am sure you will give me a fair answer. Apart from all other symptoms, or any other question, if you only find arsenic in the hair, you would take that as being a symptom of a prolonged course of arsenic?
A   Of a course of arsenic over some period.
Q   And the minimum period would be something about three months?
A   I think that.
Q   In the proximal portion but not in the distal portion. You would not expect to find it in the distal end in three months would you?
A   Not in large amounts.
Q   Not in the amount you have got here, that is a comparatively large amount for the distal end?
A   This $\frac{1}{18}$th of a grain in the distal end might possibly mean some arsenic might have been taken, perhaps a year or more ago.
Q   A year ago or more?
A   More than a year ago.

At this point Marshall Hall had achieved the point he had set out to establish. He had done it by means of perfect preparation and skilful use of his material. Let Edward Marjoribanks take up the account (*loc. cit.* p. 256):

Here, I think, Marshall Hall should have sat down. If he had, Seddon might well have gone free, and Marshall by sheer scholarship and skill in using it, would have achieved a marvellous forensic triumph. 'I had not got that part of the report in my mind' Sir William told me. 'He very nearly tied me up. I don't think I have ever been so nearly trapped as I was then — it was extraordinarily clever of him.' But unfortunately — or fortunately for the ends of justice — Marshall went on driving the point home so that the jury could not possibly mistake the importance of the admissions, and all this time his learned and brilliant antagonist was thinking hard. 'He is quite right' thought Sir William, 'if the arsenic got into the hair from the system — but I am certain that the woman died from acute arsenical poisoning, which would be surprising if she was a confirmed taker of arsenic. Could the arsenic have got into the hair by any other means?'

Before Marshall had finished giving the famous analyst a lesson in analysis, Willcox had thought of the true explanation. Miss Barrow's long hair had become contaminated by the blood-stained fluid which was dispersed all over the coffin, and in this way had become tainted with arsenic. Before he left the box he made a discreet suggestion that this was the true explanation. Marshall poured scorn on this as an afterthought, as indeed it was. 'Did you not wash the hair with all care, before making the experiment?'

That was late on the Thursday afternoon. The case now literally hung by a hair. Willcox quietly went home and thought about the matter. Then he paid a visit to his hospital, and begged a length of hair from one of his fair patients. This lovely strand of hair was then soaked in the blood-stained fluid from Miss Barrow's coffin, in which the latter's hair had been found matted at her exhumation. The experiment was then entrusted to another medical man, Dr Webster; the hair was washed just as Miss Barrow's had been, and it was found to contain arsenic just as Miss Barrow's had done. On the following Tuesday Sir William was recalled to give evidence as to this experiment. The experiment was a simple one with a successful result, which any juryman could appreciate, and the effect of Marshall's brilliant cross-examination was gone.

Eight

Re-examination

I felt a violent jolt in the rear of my vehicle. I was pushed across the road by the vehicle which had collided into me. On getting out of my car I observed that I had been hit by a double decker bus. (From the statement of a witness.)

After a witness has been effectively cross-examined it is desirable to try to correct any wrong construction which has been placed on his evidence by the cross-examination by explaining or mitigating any point which has been made against the witness, or to elicit some new feature of the witness' testimony which has arisen from the cross-examination. It has been described as the task of putting Humpty Dumpty together again, and as all the King's horses and all the King's men could not do it, you will appreciate that re-examination is often a difficult if not an impossible task. The difficulties may be summarised as follows:

(a)   You do not have a proof of evidence from the witness. You are thrown back on your knowledge of the case in general and your knowledge of the witness in particular. That makes it important for you to listen and watch your own witness under cross-examination so that you may note any points in his evidence which he evidently wants to explain or mitigate or amplify. With this regard it is useful to listen attentively to the very words used because they may give you a clue to what the witness is likely to say if his mind is redirected to the point in re-examination.

For example, there may be an echo of something he has said in his proof of evidence which will enable you to question the witness in comparative safety without the fear of making matters worse.

   (b)   As in examination in chief you may not lead the witness on facts in issue. As the points on which you will wish to re-examine are likely to be in issue, considerable skill is often required to bring the mind of the witness to the point with which you want him to deal. For example, in the Dickman case a possible re-examination on the points raised in cross-examination (see page 96 above) might have gone as follows:

Q   Do you find it easy to remember the precise day on which you learnt the name of any acquaintance or friend?

Q   Would you be able to say with accuracy the week or even the month in which you learnt the name of a friend or acquaintance unless there was a particular reason for remembering?

Q   You were asked whether you knew Nisbet's name in March?

Q   Had you any particular reason to remember precisely when you learnt his name?

Q   Was he any different in that respect from any other of your friends or acquaintances.

Yet again the technique of questioning is to question along the line of an argument. Here the argument is based on the common experience that it is virtually impossible to remember without special reason the time when you learnt a person's name. You will have noticed that this line of re-examination is off the main point made in the cross-examination which was whether the witness knew Nisbet by name by the time of the murder. He was forced after much prevarication into an admission that he did. The re-examiner cannot do much with that, but what he can do is to suggest in the minds of a jury an excuse for the prevarication.

   Take as another example the scrap-dealer case (see above at page 138). There was cross-examinaiton about motive, and it was established that the company had a huge overdraft. In re-examination the witness might have been asked such questions as these:

Q   Why did the company keep an overdraft?

Q   Was the company in financial difficulties at the time?

Q   Was any subsidiary in financial difficulties at the time?

Q   Is the company in financial difficulties now?

Q   Does the company still carry an overdraft?

Q Does it carry an overdraft for the same reason now as then, namely a cash flow problem?

Once again good practical judgment has to be used in deciding whether to re-examine at all, and if so, on what topics. As a rule of thumb it is not desirable to re-examine on trivial points. To do so merely gives them an undue prominence. The basis for effective re-examination should be a line of argument founded on facts which can be elicited from the witness which place a more favourable interpretation on the witness's evidence than has emerged in cross-examination. Munkman (*loc. cit.*, p. 128) invented a re-examination of Oscar Wilde which is worth quoting in part:

Q Now as an artist do you look upon the world as divided into good and bad, or true and false or what?
A The beautiful and the ugly.
Q How would you describe anything or anybody who repelled your artistic taste?
A As ugly.
Q Is that why you used the word ugly when my friend cross-examined you?
A Yes.
Q Why did you not tell him so at the time?
A I was shocked and agitated by the unpleasant suggestion he made.

There is one advantage that the re-examiner possesses. If the cross-examiner has opened a topic in cross-examination which was not otherwise admissible, you may re-examine on the whole topic. For example if you were precluded by the rules of evidence from examining on a conversation which the witness had with a non-witness, and the cross-examiner admissibly asks questions about it you may then re-examine on the whole of the conversation. In criminal cases defence counsel should beware of contradicting a witness in cross-examination on a small discrepancy between his statement and his testimony as he runs the risk of the statement going into evidence. (See Lord Denman's Act 1865, and the case of *R* v *Riley* (1866) F & F 964 decided by Baron Channel the following year.)

Nine

Non-Adversarial Advocacy

*I laid it down very early in my career that an advocate
should never have too many points. Concentration is
the art of argument. If you are diffuse you will be cut
up in detail; if you advance with compactness and
precision you will be irresistible.*
(Reminiscences *Henry Hawkins, Baron Brampton,
vol. 1 p. 49.*)

Frequently you will be dealing with the type of case where adversarial
advocacy, for one reason or another, is out of place. Under the Children
Act 1989 proceedings should be conducted without the confrontational
tactics which used to be used, as much as in any other field of law, in
matrimonial cases. The objection to this type of advocacy is that where
the court is seeking a solution to practical problems, in which the future
of the child is in issue, it is unhelpful, to say the least, if the parties and
their legal representatives, are seeking all the time to put the other side
in the wrong.

Where you are dealing with any case in which the real issues concern
what will happen in the future, rather than what has happened in the past,
as a general rule a non adversarial approach should be adopted.

The advocacy problem which you have to address is how to represent
your lay client's best interests and yet at the same time assist the court
by adducing evidence and advancing arguments which are of genuine
value in solving the particular problems in the case.

The question is how this specifically different approach affects the technique to be used by the advocate. It is of cardinal importance for you to bear in mind precisely what the court's objective is. Unlike the kind of case in which you are trying to unravel what has happened in the past; where both sides place a different interpretation on the evidence presented; where the detection of lies, or otherwise unreliable evidence is of paramount importance; you are in this type of case assisting the court towards a clear set of objectives. And it will often be the court, adopting an interventionist approach, which will set out clearly what it needs to know in order to make its decision.

Your approach should be to adapt the techniques which have been discussed in the previous chapters. The fundamentals; argument and not mere assertion in speeches and submissions, and framing your questions on the lines of an argument, remain the same and should be rigorously followed. The arguments in speeches and those that inform the questioning should as far as possible be based on the principles which you contend should be applied in the proceedings. The tone of your speeches and questioning should be essentially 'sweet reasonableness and light'; the aggressive and hostile, should be as carefully avoided as histrionics.

A few examples of what is meant may be useful.

Suppose an application at a directions hearing in a Family Proceedings Court. The magistrates are very keen to set down a timetable for the proceedings, which shall we say, are under s. 8 of the Children Act 1989. You are the solicitor representing the mother. She at present has the two children residing with her. The father has made the application for a residence order and the stage has been reached when it is desirable for a report to be obtained from the court welfare officer. Before the directions hearing you have found out from the solicitors representing the father that he is likely to withdraw his application for a residence order if it turns out that the court welfare officer recommends that the children should continue to reside with the mother. At the hearing it becomes apparent that the magistrates are anxious to timetable the case in such a way that you and the father's solicitor will be called upon to take and exchange statements of all witnesses to be called on either side. Your view, based on your knowledge of the likely response of the father to a welfare report favourable to the mother, is that the taking and exchange of documents will only result in the two sides becoming entrenched in adversarial positions, and a resolution of the dispute is likely to become more difficult. The magistrates on the other hand are mindful of their duty to see that no unnecessary delay occurs in the proceedings and have made it clear that they require the statements of the witnesses to be taken and exchanged within 21 days; and that the full hearing should take place seven days after the welfare officers report has been filed.

The way in which you should tackle this problem is:

(1)   Acknowledge that you too are mindful of the principle that any delay in children cases is to be avoided as a general rule.

(2)   That there are, however, exceptions to that rule; where delay is not due to drift, but planned in the interests of the children.

(3)   This is one of those cases because: it is possible that in the light of the welfare officer's report the parties may be able to resolve their differences so that no order will be the most appropriate result of the proceedings. Obviously if the parents are able to resolve their dispute that will be to the advantage of the children. If the timetable which the court is suggesting is adopted it may only serve to exacerbate the dispute with the corresponding detriment to the children. An alternative timetable is that statements in the case should be exchanged seven days after the welfare report is filed and the hearing should be seven days thereafter. In this way there will be a delay in the hearing of only seven days, with the advantage that the parties may in the meantime be able to resolve their differences.

Note.

It is difficult to see that a reasoned approach to the magistrates on these lines would fail to achieve its object. Observe particularly how the argument first makes clear that you appreciate the reasoning behind the magistrates' suggestion, but from your knowledge of the case you are able to distinguish, on valid grounds, the general principle for specific reasons. Also observe how the principles of the act, that no order should be made unless it is necessary, and the paramountcy of the children's welfare, are appropriately utilised to enforce the argument.

Take another example in a child case. This time we shall look at the kind of cross examination which may be appropriate in this type of case.

The facts are that father is seeking a residence order in respect of his child. The child is now two years old. The child's mother committed suicide a year ago, and since then the child has been living with the mother's sister and her family. This aunt and uncle to the child are happily married with children of their own and the child has settled in with them extremely well. There is clear evidence from the welfare officer that the child has changed remarkably since being placed in the aunt's family. He has blossomed, physically and emotionally. It is also the fact that the father is afforded generous and regular access to the child by the aunt and her family. The father is said to have had a stormy relationship with the mother. They separated on a number of occasions during their relationship. It is said by the aunt, whom you represent, that her sister had told her that the father was not interested in the child when he was born. The aunt believes that part of the reason for the mother's loss of confidence in herself and her abilities were due to the way in which she was treated by the father; although it is not suggested that her suicide could be attributed directly to his conduct towards her.

The father's case is that he is the best person to look after the child, being the natural parent. Although he works, he has made arrangements, should he obtain a residence order, for his mother to help him look after the child. She would be able to look after the child at all times when he would be away from home in the course of his work.

On these basic facts the question is how you, on the aunt's behalf should approach the cross examination.

The primary assumption that the court will have in mind is that the natural parent should have the care of the child unless there are positive reasons why the welfare of the child requires otherwise. The usual reasons for breaking the natural bond are to do with the inability of the natural parents to provide adequate parenting for the child in terms of his physical and emotional development. The court, therefore, is only likely to resolve the case in favour of the aunt if you can show that the father is not able to provide parenting, which to use the currently accepted phrase, 'is just good enough'.

There is not much to be gained by trying to make out that the father is not really interested in looking after the child, unless there is something positive which would make it credible that the father's application is not genuine. Similarly, there is no point in trying to explore the father's stormy relationship with the mother, for the simple reason that it is irrelevant to the issue with which the court is dealing.

You will want to concentrate on the plans which the father has made for looking after the child. The following topics should be explored:

(1)   How much time will he actually spend with the child?
(2)   How much time has his mother spent with the child up to now?
(3)   How much time will she have to spend with the child while he is at work?

(4)   Has she any other commitments?

(5)   What practical steps has he prepared in the event that his mother is unwell?

(6)   What are his plans for schooling and possibly religious upbringing?

(7)   What plans has he for enabling the child to see his aunt and her family?

(8)   Has he a present intention of marrying. If so, has his fiancé any experience with children and has she established any relationship with the child?

There may be many other topics which would suggest themselves from the particular circumstances of the case; but I hope I have said enough to indicate the approach which ought to be made.

The next point to consider is the form which the questions should take.

Let me take topics 1 and 2 by way of illustration.

The following probing questions might be asked.

—Where do you work?

—What are your hours of work?

—Do you work on Saturdays?

—Does your work take you away from home overnight?

—What is the longest time you have had to spend away from home?

—Is there any prospect of your workplace changing in the foreseeable future?

—What are your prospects with your present company?

—How much holiday are you allowed each year?

—Has the child been living continuously with his aunt for the last year?

—Has the child ever spent the night at your mother's?

—On how many occasions?

—When was the last time?

—How long did he stay?

—Were you there all the time?

—How long were you away?

—Was your mother in hospital late last year?

—What was the matter?

—Does she have to return to hospital for check ups?

—Will she have to be admitted?

—What steps will you take to look after the child if your company requires you to move to a different part of the country?

—How could your mother afford to follow you?

Notes.

(1)   All these questions are designed to elicit information. What is being sought is information which the court needs to make its decision.

(2)   The tone of the questions, while firm, is entirely in keeping with the search for information. There is no hint of hostility. It could as well be an examination in chief.

(3)   Each topic is dealt with fully before passing to the next.

(4)   The order in which you deal with your topics will depend on your perception of what clarity of presentation requires. This order should usually be left to the 'feel' of the case at the time of questioning. If in doubt keep to a logical order.

It is important for every advocate to bear in mind the President's *Practice Direction* of 31 January 1995 which follows the practice directions handed down by the Lord Chief Justice and the Vice Chancellor to apply in the Queen's Bench and Chancery Divisions. The President's direction applies in all care centres, family hearing centres and divorce county courts.

The direction is headed 'case management'. Paragraph 1 states: 'The importance of reducing the cost and delay of civil litigation makes it necessary for the Court to assert greater control over the preparation for and conduct of hearings than has hitherto been customary. Failure by practitioners to conduct cases economically will be visited by appropriate orders for cost, including wasted costs orders.'

This new departure should be regarded for our purposes as a guide to the new style of advocacy which should now be followed in the courts. It is plain that the prolix advocacy which has developed since the last war has to be curbed. The order of the day is to be brief, clear and above all relevant.

Paragraph 2 states:

The Court will accordingly exercise its discretion to limit—

(a)   Discovery.

(b)   The length of opening and closing submissions:

(c)   The time allowed for the examination and cross-examination of witnesses:

(d)   The issues on which it wishes to be addressed:

(e)   Reading aloud from documents and authorities.

Each of these points is worthy of discussion.

(a) *Discovery*. The problem of appropriate discovery is one of the
most intractable in present day litigation. Particularly since the criminal
case of *Ward*, it has become the practice for there to be very detailed and
extensive discovery in every type of litigation where there is likely to be
documentation in the hands of third parties as well as the parties to the
action. The object of such discovery is that it is thought to be in the
interests of justice that everything which might conceivably be relevant
to achieving a just result should be known to the parties. The notorious
Matrix Churchill case, which gave rise to the Scott Enquiry, is a case in
point. Such cases are plain enough, but many are not so plain. What
practical limits should be placed on discovery? How will the judges'
discretion be exercised in limiting discovery? In the context of this
chapter, what is the role of the advocate in responsibly assisting the court
in ordering the discovery which is needed to do justice?

The advocates need to know what the real issues in the case are and
the law which applies to them. Nothing less will do; for how else can they
know what will be relevant to disclose. If the advocate on one side does
not really know what the other party's case is, he should do all that is
practicable to find out. More and more frequently nowadays the court will
require the advocates to get together to hammer out what the real issues
are; the earlier that is done in the proceedings the better. There is less and
less prospect of the courts countenancing, let alone encouraging, the
highly tactical use of procedures to ambush the other side.

(b) *The length of opening and closing oral submissions.* This part of
the direction is aimed, no doubt, at the advocate who does not seem to
know what is relevant or irrelevant; and who will insist on going through
a crude alphabet of the case. To avoid this tendency — and few, even of
the best, have not indulged it from time to time — requires self-discipline
and hard work. It also requires the confidence which assures you that you
are dealing with what really matters. Lengthy speeches are often
defensive in the sense that the advocate is not quite sure what is important
and what is not. It is based on the notion that the judge may think you
have a good point, even if you yourself do not think much of it. Use your
own good discretion to solve this dilemma. You will sometimes make
errors of judgement, but by practice and hard thinking you will reduce
them to a minimum.

(c) *The time allowed for the examination and cross-examination of
witnesses.* Much the same considerations apply as set out in (b). It is
important for the advocate to choose with acumen what points to examine
and cross-examine. When the points have been chosen they should be

dealt with fully and carefully on the lines suggested in other parts of this book. If you are doing the job properly there is little likelihood of your being stopped by the impatient judge, simply because you will not be taxing the judge's patience. Or is that a too complacent view of the patience of judges? Perhaps it is. If it is, and the judge appears to invade your rights as an advocate, then you must stand up for your rights in the confidence that you know your duty as well as the judge knows his.

(d) *The issues on which it wishes to be addressed.* The shrewd advocate will have forseen what those issues are likely to be and will have prepared the relevant submissions. If, however, you have overlooked an aspect of the case which the judge thinks is important, you must be candid with the court. Say that you have not given the point proper consideration, and if necessary ask for a short adjournment to consider it.

(e) *Reading aloud from documents and authorities.* Effective advocacy often requires the art of summarising the effect of documents or authorities. It is time-consuming but well worth the effort. The difficulty is to select what really matters and to omit the rest; and yet not to distort what is said in the document or authority by over-simplification or brevity. Practice, as usual, improves one's skill.

Paragraph 3 provides:

Unless otherwise ordered, every witness statement or affidavit shall stand as the evidence in chief of the witness concerned. The substance of the evidence which a party intends to adduce at the hearing must be sufficiently detailed, but without prolixity; it must be confined to material issues of fact, not (except in the case of the evidence of professional witnesses) of opinion; and if hearsay evidence is to be adduced, the source of the information must be declared or good reason given for not doing so.

This part of the direction places a responsibility on the advocate to advise on evidence. Particular attention will have to be paid to the following points: What are the real issues? Have they been adequately dealt with in the proposed draft of evidence? What irrelevant matters have been included and which ought to be excised?

It may happen in some cases that it is necessary to seek leave at a directions hearing to adduce oral evidence in examination in chief in addition to the statement or affidavit. There must be a cogent reason for seeking leave; but there may be certain categories of evidence which might properly be the subject of additional oral evidence. There may be evidence which is likely to become available only at the last minute because of a developing situation, or in response to something said on the other side. The direction does not seek to set out the circumstances in which leave may be given — they are likely to be infinitely variable — but the advocate should be on the alert to see that all relevant evidence is adduced, even if it means applying for leave for it to be given orally.

Under paragraph 4:

It is a duty owed to the court both by the parties and by their legal representatives to give full and frank disclosure in ancillary relief applications and also in all matters in respect of children. The parties and their advisers must also use their best endeavours:

(a)   to confine the issues and the evidence called to what is reasonably considered to be essential for the proper presentation of their case;

(b)   to reduce or eliminate issues for expert evidence;

(c)   in advance of the hearing to agree which are the issues or the main issues.

The necessity for full disclosure is an endorsement of the case law. In getting at the issues in the case there should now be no inhibition about revealing every aspect of the case on which you rely at the stage when, for example, expert evidence is exchanged. I believe that in all cases, whether criminal or civil, there will in future be required a much greater level of discussion between the legal advisers of the parties before final hearing. Take, for example, facts from which two sets of proceedings arise; criminal and family. It is alleged that a small child has been caused really serious bodily harm by her stepfather. Criminal proceedings are begun against him. At the same time the local authority begin care proceedings. The care proceedings are transferred from the Family Proceedings Court to the care centre.

At the care centre at the first directions hearing a time table is set down which includes a final hearing date; say in three months. Meanwhile the criminal proceedings are also progressing. At the plea and directions hearing the trial date is fixed to take place two months before the final hearing in the family case. But then the defence in the criminal proceedings seek an adjournment because they want to obtain expert evidence on the question of how the injuries were caused to the child. At the time of the application to adjourn there are in the care proceedings two experts' reports. The first deals with the state in which the child presented at hospital on the date of the alleged offence. The second deals with the alleged causation based on an examination of the child, on x-rays and on the facts set out in the first report.

Meanwhile for the criminal proceedings a report is obtained by the prosecution from a pathologist which states that a theory of causation propounded by an expert instructed on behalf of the defendant in the criminal proceedings is untenable. The defence wish to obtain the view of another expert to deal with the pathologist's report. They say that it will take some months to obtain. It will undoubtedly run beyond the date for hearing in the care proceedings.

Because of the urgency of the care proceedings it is necessary to avoid, if at all possible, any adjournment of the final hearing in the care case.

This is a situation where it is essential that the prosecution and the defence pool their resources to make sure:

(a)   that all relevant reports are submitted to the expert instructed by the defence without any delay;
(b)   that the defence expert is called upon to provide his report within a strict time limit, in this case to enable the original trial date to be kept.

If necessary, a court order should be obtained to achieve that objective.

From this illustration it will be appreciated that the legal advisers on both sides will be called upon to play a vital role in keeping the proceedings moving. At the same time, by candid discussion and exchange of information, they concentrate on the essential issues.

Paragraph 5 of the direction deals with the bundling of documents. I have already dealt with this question and nothing needs to be added by way of comment here.

Paragraphs 6 and 7 deal with pre-trial listing arrangements and with the provision of skeleton arguments. They need no further elaboration for the purposes of this discussion.

Paragraph 8 states: 'In advance of the hearing upon request, and otherwise in course of their opening, parties should be prepared to furnish the court, if there is no core bundle, with a list of documents essential for a proper understanding of the case.' Here again we have a demand for careful preparation by the advocate. This requirement ties in with the preparation of skeleton arguments.

Under paragraph 9: 'The opening speech should be succinct. At its conclusion other parties may be invited briefly to amplify their skeleton arguments. In a heavy case the court may in conjunction with final speeches require written submissions, including the findings of fact for which each party contends.' The emphasis here is on the brevity of oral submissions. It may be assumed that in making written submissions the advocate will be as short as the circumstances allow. The only way in which these demands can effectively be met is to concentrate on the essential issues of fact and law.

Paragraph 10 deals with the application of the direction and requires no comment.

Ten

The Personality of the Advocate

> *The mark of a truly civilized man is confidence in the*
> *strength and security derived from the inquiring mind.*
> *(Frankfurter J.)*

In the preceding pages the technique of speech making and questioning
has been discussed and illustrated, but very little has been said about
developing your personality as an advocate; creating a favourable
atmosphere in Court and knowing when to speak and when to be silent.

Aristotle referred to the three elements in a speech. The speaker, the
contents of the speech and the audience. The personality of the speaker is
of equal importance with the other two. Lord Birkett in his essay on the
Art of Advocacy (*Six Great Advocates*, Penguin, p. 105) had this to say:

When James Russell Lowell recalled the eloquence of the spoken word
of Emerson, he said:

Was never eye did see that face,
Was never ear did hear that tongue,
Was never mind did mind his grace
That ever thought the travail long;
But eyes and ears and every thought
Were with his sweet perfections caught.

It was the distinctive quality of personality that gave the compelling
power to Emerson's speaking, and all the great advocates I have

known and all the great orators I have heard had this great and indispensible quality.... The effect achieved depends on the character and quality of the speaker himself, the occasion on which he speaks, the subject-matter of the speech and the form in which the speech is cast. It is sometimes said that the whole art of advocacy consists in presentation.... Voice, gesture, knowledge, language, emotion — all go into the art of presentation.

... If the all important task of the advocate is to persuade ... there are certain things that the ordinary run of advocates do well to observe. Whatever the case and whatever the court, the first and vital thing is that the advocate shall know the case he desires to make with complete thoroughness. He must have a complete mastery of the facts and he must have the power to present them in the most attractive way. He must have a quick mind and an understanding heart. He must acquire in some way an insight into human nature and a natural and unforced sympathy with all sorts and conditions of men. Above all, he must have what I can only call an intuitive recognition of what the circumstances of the case require as it slowly unfolds itself before the court.

Lord Birkett thus sets out the standards which the aspiring advocate may one day hope to achieve; and it is helpful, though perhaps daunting, to have a standard to aim for.

At the outset it is useful for you to learn to listen to yourself. You should learn if you can, to be self critical. You should watch carefully the effect your speech has on your audience; see whether you speak too fast or labour your delivery; note whether the tribunal follows your argument; if so, how you achieved that degree of clarity, if not, what went wrong.

It is obvious, on a moment's consideration, that everything about you contributes to the impression you make as an advocate. Appearance, deportment, delivery, gesture, good manners ('the shadows of virtue' as Sydney Smith called them), good humour and wit should all be cultivated in the presentation of yourself as an advocate; and above all art must conceal art. There is nothing worse in advocacy than affectation.

There are some people who are born with a personality which carries all before them, but most of us have to cultivate what talents we have. To a great extent we do so unconsciously, imitating those we admire in some trick or feature, and gradually by a process of accretion we mould our own personalities. The advocate may well wish to use this process consciously, deliberately borrowing from many others aspects of personality to incorporate in his own — in short, artfully cultivating his own style.

The insight into human nature of which Lord Birkett spoke is no doubt acquired in all sorts of ways, but you can hasten the results of experience and the revelations of intuition by the deliberate noting of how people behave, in the same way as novelists do.

The hallmark of the very best advocates is that they make very few mistakes. Their judgment is always sure; it is founded upon full knowledge of the facts; an ability to see and weigh opposing arguments; to distinguish between the reality and the shadow, and so on. You can improve your judgment by self-criticism, by discussion with friends and colleagues, and by reading, especially history and biography. As an advocate you never know when a piece of knowledge is going to prove of value; wide reading and practical knowledge of the world are necessary equipment for the advocate whatever his sphere of work.

I should like to end with a comment on the ethics of advocacy. The point was excellently made by Lord Macmillan in an essay on the Art of Advocacy, *Law and Other Things*, Cambridge University Press, 1937, p. 200:

There are some who would malign the art of the advocate as dishonest and morally degrading. The taunt is as old as Plato, and so is its refutation. There is no calumny more unfounded. It is an art truly beset with perils but there is no sphere in which gifts of character and uprightness are more sure of recognition and reward. It has been practised by some of the noblest men in the long and glorious annals of our country. Practised with a high sense of honour which has always characterised the Bar in our country, it is the sure bulwark of justice and liberty. 'I for one', says Quintilian, 'restrict the name of orator and the art itself to those who are good'.

That was written in 1933. The Bar since then has much expanded; rights of audience have been given to the other branch of the profession and more and more solicitors will no doubt exercise those rights. In 1933 the number of women practising at the Bar was very small. Now the numbers of women succeeding in the two branches of the profession increase year by year; and no one would deny that the profession has been immensely strengthened. But the argument in Lord Macmillan's remarks is just as valid and equally relevant as it was more than 50 years ago.

Eleven

Do's and Don'ts

What sort of argument is most effective in an appellate court? Shall it be long or short, terse or discursive? Shall it assume that the judges know the rudiments of law or shall it attempt in a brief hour to supply the defects in their early training? Shall it state the law or the facts? Shall it take up the authorities and analyse them, or shall it content itself with conclusions and leave analysis for the study? There is of course no universal formula which will fit all situations in appellate courts or elsewhere. If I had, however, to prepare a list of don'ts for the guidance of the novice, I think I would say that only in the rarest cases is it wise to take up one decision after another for the purpose of dissection. Such autopsies have their value at times, but they are wearisome and gruesome scenes. In my list of don'ts I would add, don't state the minutiae of the evidence. The judges won't follow you, and if they followed would forget. Don't attempt to supplement the defects of early training. Your auditors are hardened sinners, not easily redeemed. Above all, don't be long winded. I have in mind a lawyer ... whose arguments lasted about a quarter of an hour. He told us his point and sat down. The audience at the rear of the courtroom might not applaud, but the audience

in front did — at least in spirit — and since the latter
audience has the votes, it is best to make your play for
them. (Benjamin N. Cardozo, 1868–1938, Justice of
the Supreme Court of the United States)

General preparation

At the outset decide what you must prove and disprove. Look for the facts which tell in your favour and those against you. Consider the law applicable to the case as early as possible in your preparation; that is, when you have identified the issues. Make a note of the authorities or statutes you consult during your preparation, even if you reject what you have just read as not being immediately relevant. It may become relevant as preparation proceeds and you may save yourself considerable time if you can turn it up again immediately.

Read all the papers and documentary exhibits. Do not be content with a summary or leave to the discretion of those instructing you what you should be shown. Ask to see everything, and make sure, as far as you are able, that you are shown everything.

Always look at the exhibits carefully. You may see something that others have not noticed. For example, in a fraud case, where there were thousands of exhibits, there was one document which showed that a defendant had been a director of a company for a few days. Significantly he had resigned on the day after he had been interviewed by the police. Defence counsel did not notice the document, or if he did, forgot it. In the result the defendant said in his evidence in chief that he had never been a director of that company. When the lie was exposed by counsel for the prosecution in cross-examination, the defendant's credibility was badly damaged. Had the defence counsel dealt with it in chief, the damage could have been greatly weakened, if not nullified altogether.

Always look at the back of documentary exhibits. You will be surprised at what you will sometimes find.

In cases of sexual assault always inquire of the prosecution whether the complainant has made similar complaints on previous occasions.

Visit the scene of the incident; look at the machinery on site which gave rise to the accident; look for yourself, if practicable, at the scene where the road accident occurred, etc.

Understand maps, plans, diagrams etc., early on in your preparation. If in doubt have them explained by the expert if you intend to call one.

Always prepare a chronology of the salient facts. You will often find that it can be used as the framework for your presentation of the case.

Even if you are not called on to write an advice on evidence you should for your own purposes appraise the state of the evidence frequently as you proceed in your preparation of a large case. In the run of the mill case you should make at least one appraisal in time to seek any new evidence required.

Make sure that all the statements and documents with which you have been provided have page numbers. This will enable you to cross-reference with ease. If you cannot dictate the order in which statements are drawn up, or documents exhibited, consult your opponent as soon as possible to see if your page numbers and his are the same. It can be very unsettling if you arrive at court only to find that all your preparation, notes, and cross-referencing has been done with different pagination from that provided to the court.

When you have selected the authorities you wish to cite, make sure that you flag the pages to which you may wish to refer and place the books or photostats in the order in which you intend to refer to them on the desk.

Preparation of your speeches

Identify the argument which you intend to present. Think out its logical sequence. Note the skeleton of the argument. Always think of your tribunal in deciding what you will include and omit. Your aim should be to present the case with maximum clarity and at the same time to arouse and maintain the interest of your listeners.

If you can, discuss with a friend difficult points in your argument. When you go into Court your mind should be seething with your material.

Always strive for accurate statement of fact. Misquotation of evidence, misstatement of the law and erroneous inferences can damage the presentation of your case, sometimes irrevocably. In this context you should, if for example you are quoting from literature, quote accurately. If your judges know the quotation themselves they will be irritated by your getting it wrong, when they may have been charmed if you had got it right.

When you are replying to an opponent's speech do not, save perhaps in very exceptional circumstances, deal with his speech point by point. It is fighting him on ground of his choosing. In effect he is dictating the pace and the intensity of the argument. The temptation to answer point by point is often based on the misapprehension that there are only two sides to an argument. More often there are many sides to a question all of which, in some sense, may be said to be right. The point is well illustrated when dissenting speeches are made in the House of Lords. You may often find that the majority view when compared with the dissenting view is reached by looking at the undisputed facts or law from a different standpoint: yet both standpoints can be said to be objectively right.

Let the strength of your argument as a whole despatch your opponent's argument, but as you develop your argument you may strike many a shrewd blow at detailed points in your opponent's.

Always argue: never merely assert without giving reasons.

Aim to be brief and to the point. Don't waffle: don't expatiate on the obvious and elaborate on the self-evident. Don't repeat yourself unless you are sure that you have not been understood; and if you must repeat yourself, do it artfully.

By all means use wit and humour in your speaking, but be sure as far as you can be, that you can carry it off before you try it. Distinguish wit and humour from mere flippancy; flippancy is usually out of place in court.

Always, if you can, be good humoured. However ardent you are in your cause, be averse to quarrel either with your opponent or the judge.

If, as sometimes happens, the judge improperly invades the rights of your client, or your rights as an advocate, it is necessary to stand up to him. Don't be sycophantic, but be polite. Respect the office of a judge if you cannot respect the judge himself. It was said of the first Lord Russell of Killowen:

> that he would not hesitate for a moment to stand up to any judge, and if the need arose, to address the judge with vehemence if he thought the rights of the advocate were being invaded. He once addressed some angry and rather violent words to Mr Justice Denman, who said that he could not trust himself to reprove Russell that night because of his sorrow and resentment, but would adjourn the court and consider what to do next morning. But next morning when the learned judge began to refer to 'the painful incident' of the previous night, Russell broke in and said 'Do not say a further word, my Lord, for I have forever dismissed it from my mind'. The crowded court dissolved in laughter at this bold and unexpected intervention and even the judge joined in. But I know of no other advocate who would have dared to reprove the judge at night and then appear to forgive him in the morning! [Lord Birkett in his essay on Sir Charles Russell QC in *Six Great Advocates* Penguin, p. 71]

Pay close attention to the way in which you express yourself. Remember that the telling phrase, the apt quotation, the vivid illustration lingers in the memory of your listeners and influences judgment. And be fastidious in your choice of language to the end that you express exactly what you mean.

Don't use cliches. They are a substitute for thought. As a general rule don't use slang; but if a slang word or an everyday colloquialism expresses your meaning better than any alternative, use it.

Don't speak too fast. Pace yourself so that the tribunal is able to follow without discomfort; but don't be too slow either. A varied pace is best, designed to suit the sense of what you are saying.

Never express your own opinion, even inferentially: 'You may have believed that witness, members of the jury, but I'll be horrified if you do.'

Always be clear, but do not be boringly and pedantically clear; nor should you leave nothing to be inferred. There is a point at which clarity ceases to be a virtue.

Of questioning

Examination in Chief   At the outset try to put the witness at ease by a few non-controversial and easy questions. The witness will then have a chance of getting used to the atmosphere of the court and the sound of his own voice there.

Aim to elicit the evidence you want from the witness as though in a conversation in which you are playing the subordinate role. In fact you should be exercising complete control over the witness by the use of precise questions.

Don't, save in very exceptional circumstances, give the witness a free reign: 'Just tell us in your own words what happened'; this merely invites at best a rambling and extensive account or a crude alphabet of the topic, or at worst the admission of evidence which is irrelevant, inadmissible or damaging to your case.

Always ask but one question at a time. Make it as sharp as possible so that it demands an answer dictated by the terms in which it is asked.

Ask the question directly without preamble. Don't make comments within the form of the question, at least not so that you will attract criticism for doing so.

Don't get cross with the witness even if you think him obtuse, or difficult or rude.

Always listen carefully to the answer to the question. That may sound too obvious to state when you read it in cold print, but often the inexperienced are so concerned to think of the next question that they plough on regardless. Listen particularly for the nuances of the answer: and watch for the effect of the answers on the tribunal.

Be sure not to use words which the witness may not understand. Don't say 'prior to' when you mean 'before', 'apprehend' when you mean 'understand', or 'transpired that' when you mean 'happened', 'occurred', or 'turned out'.

If the witness cannot remember a crucial point, leave it and come back to it later. The best way of avoiding this difficulty is to adopt a chronological order in dealing with the incident about which the witness is speaking. Alternatively you may have noticed in the witness' proof of evidence, or in conference that the witness refers to a piece of evidence out of sequence. If so, deal with it in that odd order when the witness is giving evidence, because it often happens that you get something into your head and before you can get it out you have to unlearn it. Be on the look out for some striking word or incident in the witness' proof which is likely to jog his memory; you can then introduce it into your question (without leading of course).

If your witness gives you a damaging answer don't betray your disappointment by grimace or gesture, but carry on as though it was just the answer you expected.

Cross-Examination   Form a hypothesis which accommodates all the known facts of the case. This will define the boundaries of your cross-examination and prevent you from straying unwittingly into uncharted territory.

Base your questions on the lines of an argument, but do not follow the logical order of the argument in asking your questions if to do so would disable the effectiveness of the examination in any way.

Always keep your questions short; press for an answer to the question in the terms in which it is asked.

Don't allow the witness to evade the question. Repeat it if necessary.

Deal with each topic completely before passing on to the next, unless you have a cogent reason for departing from this general rule.

If you propose to drive a witness into a corner prevent him from seeing the drift of your questions for as long as possible. You can do this in numerous ways. For example, you can approach the point stealthily by establishing essential points in your argument out of order, so that it is unlikely that anyone will see the point of the question at the time it is asked. When you do this it may happen that the judge, anxious to get on, will get fidgety and ask you the relevance of the question. Don't be unnerved: pacify him tactfully without giving the point away. Most judges will get the point and will be sorry they interrupted, especially if you are doing your job competently. Another servicable device is to ask the crucial question as though it were no more than an afterthought. An example of this is to be found in the celebrated cross-examination of Piggott by Sir Charles Russell in the *Parnell* case; He wanted to see if Piggott spelt the word 'hesitancy', 'hesitency', as it was spelt wrongly in the forged letters. He asked him to write out a number of words of no significance. He then said: 'There is one word I had forgotten. Lower down please, leaving spaces, write the word 'hesitancy' with a small h'.

The apparent afterthought, the instructions, and the insistence on the small 'h' were all designed to distract the witness' attention from the spelling of the word so that he would be likely to spell it as he usually did. Sure enough he spelt it with an 'e' rather than an 'a' just as the forger had done.

When you are trying to get the witness to commit himself to a particular proposition or propositions do not supply the answer in the form of your question. If you do so you relieve the pressure on the witness. He should be forced to commit himself to each proposition before proceeding to the next point. (The 'I will level with you' cross-examination is a good example of this at page 122.) Supplying the answer is a very common fault and requires firm discipline not to do it.

When you are forcing the witness to adopt a position it is often useful and necessary to go into precise detail. You may, for example, want to contrast this witness' account of the detail with the next witness' in order to throw up discrepancies; again it may be that you want to show how the witness' evidence does not dovetail with the reality when the detail is examined.

It is a good rule of thumb to avoid asking the question 'Are you sure'. It is often used as a fill-in question while the examiner is thinking of the next question after being flummoxed by the answer which has just been given. It is sometimes used to underline the fact that the witness has committed himself to a particular proposition, but that is unwise. If the witness is intelligent he may, on being asked if he is sure, guess that he is being trapped and start trying to resile from what he has just said. Rather than use this question it is better to ask questions on circumstantial detail, as in the 'seal on the will' cross-examination at page 111.

When you want to bring a witness under great pressure and allow him as little opportunity for invention as possible, ask your questions rapidly and keep them as short and sharp as possible.

Be careful how you use sarcasm in cross-examination. While it can be a useful weapon in your armoury it should be used with the guiding principle of questioning fairly in mind.

Use probing questions to:

(a) Make a witness commit himself to a particular account.

(b) Acquire information from the witness.

(c) Test the evidence of the witness with who, why, what, when where, and how.

Use insinuation to:

(a) Put your case.

(b) Draw the witness on into accepting an alternative interpretation of the facts.

(c) Confront the witness with a damaging and unassailable fact.

Never cross-examine without a particular end in view.

Never ask unnecessary questions.

When you have got what you need, stop. An excellent maxim for the cross-examiner is that better is the enemy of good.

Never get involved in a personal ding-dong with the witness. If he asks you a question, evade it by some such answer that it is not for the witness to ask you questions.

Never be gratuitously rude to the witness. A severe but polite cross-examination tends to avoid the feeling in the tribunal that the witness is the underdog.

Don't cross-examine on niggling discrepancies which, taking a reasonable view of the facts as a whole, make little or no difference: 'You said in your statement that your father died when he was 72, but you said just now that he was about 72. Now which is it?' This sort of question when it is of no moment, although correct, only serves to damage your case because your tribunal will gain the impression that you have no better material.

Don't interrupt a witness who is trying to answer your question. It will give the impression that you are being unfair, or that you dislike the answer you are getting.

Use a surprise question to knock the witness off-balance.

Always be wary lest your cross-examination lets in damaging evidence in re-examination which would otherwise be inadmissible. This requires a full and clear working knowledge of the rules of evidence.

Of re-examination

Bring the witness's mind to the point which you want him to deal with
by leading questions when they are permissible, following as far as you
can the order which is likely to bring the witness to deal with the point
naturally. You should not go to the point direct: 'You remember you said
in cross-examination that you thought the radio was stolen property when
Soapy Joe handed it to you. Will you explain what you meant?' This
makes it very difficult for the witness to think out what he really wants
to say, because it is without warning. It is better done like this:

Q   You told us you met Soapy at the Bull that night?
A   Yes, I did.
Q   Had you met him before that night?
A   Never.
Q   Did you know that he was a crook at the time you spoke to him?
A   No, I did not.
Q   When did you first learn that he was?
A   When the police told me that night at the police station.
Q   It is agreed that the policeman said to you 'You must have known the
      radio was stolen because Soapy is a well-known thief.' Before the
      officer said that to you, did you know that Soapy was a thief?
A   No, I certainly did not.
Q   At the time you bought the radio from him, did you know or believe
      that it was stolen?
A   I would not have bought it if I had.
Q   When you said in cross-examination that you thought the radio was
      stolen when Soapy handed it to you, what did you mean?
A   Well, I meant that when the police told me Soapy was a thief I thought
      the radio was stolen because Soapy had handed it to me.

General aids to good advocacy

Get to Court with plenty of time to spare. Make sure that you look neat
and tidy. A slovenly appearance is likely to distract attention from what
you are saying.

Make sure that you speak clearly. It is irritating to the listener if you
are on the fringe of audibility, as too many advocates are.

Stand still when you are speaking and don't fidget. Do not, for
example, hold a piece of tape in your hands; you are sure to start winding
and unwinding it. This can be very distracting for your listeners.

Keep your papers in good order throughout the case. You should be able to turn up what you want promptly.

Pace yourself. Do not rush on without regard to whether the judge has found the page to which you have just referred him.

Try to have as much of the case in your head as possible, because if you are free of your notes you can watch the impression you are making on the tribunal so much more carefully.

If you have two good points and five which are indifferent, concentrate on the two good ones and ignore the others which only serve to confuse or detract from the presentation of the good points.

Many times it happens that you have a hopeless case to present, and the longer it continues the worse it seems to get. You should remain undismayed. You should be on the look out for any slip which your opponent may make and take legitimate advantage of it. You should argue every genuine point to best effect; your impression of the weakness of the case may be mistaken and a point which does not appeal to you may appeal to the judge. Sometimes an unforeseen point may emerge which wholly changes the complexion of the case. In civil cases it is sometimes possible, by a good tactical concession to salvage something from the case, even if it is only costs.

Finally, approach every case in the same conscientious way, whether it is big or small, important or trivial.

Appendix 1

Sir Patrick Hastings Final Speech in Defence of Mr Morland

In July 1931, Lord Kylsant was charged with fraud. Mr Morland, the company auditor, was jointly charged with him on two counts. It was alleged that Lord Kylsant had used his virtually dictatorial powers to have balance sheets issued by the company which misled the public and that Mr Morland had connived at the deception.

Sir Patrick Hastings appeared for the defence of Morland. His final speech was as follows:

If your Lordship pleases: members of the jury: there is one matter I particularly want to mention to you, because I omitted it in the observations I made to you yesterday [his opening speech for the defence], and I think it is a matter which is really worthy of your consideration, as a pure question of fact. Except for the moment when the Clerk of the Court read out the charge, I am not quite sure that it has been brought home to your minds that the charge against my client Mr Morland, is that of being an accessory or aider to Lord Kylsant in that which it is suggested he has done. The point may, I think, become clear when the Attorney-General addresses you, but at the moment I confess it is not quite clear to me. I am not quite clear what it is that Mr Morland is suggested to have done. Is it that he put in the words 'adjustment of taxation reserves', or is it something else? Because if so it is a little odd. He certainly did not aid Lord Kylsant to put those words into the document, because Lord Kylsant did not want them in at all, or he did not care whether they were in or not. Mr Morland alone put in those words. I still remain, as I have been all along, a little puzzled to know exactly what it is that is suggested against Mr Morland. His evidence was quite clear. It is entirely a matter for you but I would have thought he said it quite frankly, he said: 'I often make suggestions, but only after very careful thought. When I make them, I expect them to be carried out. I made this one'.

The Attorney-General quite fairly pressed him to know whether he would have signed the balance sheet without them, and he said: 'I do not quite know, but if I make a decision I want it carried out, and if it is not carried out I have to consider very carefully whether I will sign the balance sheet at all'. If Mr Morland did that nobody could suggest that he aided Lord Kylsant to put these words in, because he put them in himself and Lord Kylsant had nothing whatever to do with it. Members of the jury, when one considers whether or not those words make the balance sheet better or worse, one must remember this — I understand the suggestion is that without these words this balance sheet would be misleading, but these words in themselves are not sufficient. The Attorney-General said: 'If you had put that which appears in the year 1928 'crediting income tax reserves' that would have been sufficient'. You and I are in the same position as the Attorney-General, and indeed for this purpose we may all take our own views. You may take the view that the Attorney-General is right or wrong, when he suggests that the words 'crediting transfers from the reserves' would be better than 'adjustments'. You may take the view that it makes no difference. Anyone may make such an assumption: but the question surely that we are considering here is what is the proper meaning to be given to every word that Mr Morland has used. I do not want to go back and read to you the evidence again, but does it not strike you as odd that no single witness has ever suggested that these words were misleading. The only persons we have had an opportunity of calling with regard to that were members of a profession which is accustomed to deal with accounts and balance sheets, and there has not been the slightest divergence of opinion. [He then cites the various witnesses.] Is it quite fair that there should remain, at least in this case, this theory that the words that everybody says are the right words — witnesses alike for the prosecution and the defence — and which were deliberately chosen by Mr Morland because they were the right words — is it quite fair that they should be criticised now? If the learned Attorney-General's view is right that the words we have in this case 'adjustments of taxation reserves', are misleading, one cannot help pointing out that, if you look at the balance sheet, which he says is right, and if you look at the quotations after its issue, they are equally constant with those that appear the day before. I do not know if the suggestion is that these words 'adjustment of taxation reserves' are right for an accountant, but not for an ordinary member of the public. There is not a particle of evidence, not a document, there is nothing or any living soul who says that this gentleman has done anything wrong. On the contrary, everybody, whether you go to the witnesses for the defence, whether you go to the witnesses for the prosecution, whether you go to the voice of the public as appearing in the documents printed at the time, they all say he did right.

If the suggestion is this, that the whole balance sheet in its essence ought to have told the shareholders, through Mr Morland or with his help, that this company would fail unless trade improved, my only answer to that is, just as I said before, every witness who has been asked says frankly: 'If I had been in the position of Mr Morland, I would have done exactly the same as he did: I would have said nothing'. These gentlemen admitted that they would have signed the balance sheet. No gentleman who holds a great public position is going into the witness box to commit perjury. If he did so, he would be a figure of scorn to those who trusted him and helped to put him in the position he occupied. How can they say Mr Morland has done anything wrong? What has he done? What does Sir William M'Lintock say he has done? The Attorney-General no doubt may have some explanation to give you of something that Mr Morland has done wrong, but it is in the face of the heads of the accountancy profession: it is in the face of Lord Plender: it is in the face of Mr Hill and Mr Morgan who have sworn on oath that they themselves would have done the thing for which this gentleman is standing there in the dock.

Members of the jury, some time ago I suggested that if this action was to result in a verdict against this gentleman you could not get a dock big enough to hold all the accountants who should be tried. I have not got the experience that many people have in this court. There are members of the Bar who practise habitually in this Court, who are here every day and who see and are accustomed to see men standing in the dock. Quite frankly I am not. I have been wondering since I have been here whether they are not a little apt to forget what we are doing. We are really trying a man for his life. It is life and death to Mr Morland to be sitting where he is sitting. To me (I do not know what it is to you) it is an unbelievable horror that night after night, when we have gone home from here, we might have thought: 'Here is this gentleman, a man who has held his head as high as anyone in the City, who night after night is only allowed to leave his chair by the permission of the law let out by warders'. What can Mr Morland have done which makes it necessary that when he goes back every night he must know: 'When I wake up in the morning, I am surrendering into the custody of warders who will keep me there until I am released by permission of the Court'.

Sir John Simon said that the case to him is a great responsibility. I agree. To me it is such an awful responsibility that I have struggled to find what point I can deal with and what I can say to help you and him. I can find merely this. There is a gentleman who has, I am told, one of the greatest qualifications, namely, a good record. Mr Morland is a man who has walked the streets of London, proud of his career, proud of the fact that he could sit beside Sir Gilbert Garnsey and other members of his firm, and beside Mr Hill and Lord Plender at meetings, and chairmen of companies, and everyone of them has been proud and honoured to sit beside him, just as I tell you frankly that I and Mr Bevan and Mr Conway are proud to represent him. We have struggled to find what it is we have to deal with and what is suggested he has done. You have got at this moment Mr Morland's whole career and whole future. If you think he is guilty of a crime you will say so; but if you think, as I ask you to think, that he came into this box a respected and honest man, and if you think he should go out of that box just as respected and just as honoured, that also you should say.

I cannot help you any more, members of the jury, except in conclusion to say this. The view I put before you is that it must have been years ago, if ever, when into that box stepped a man of the position of Mr Morland, who has sat there listening to the case against himself, in a case where he is still wondering what it is. It must be years and years before ever again such a man will go into the box, and I can only beg of you not to be the first jury to say that a man such as Mr Morland must be convicted of a crime.

Notes.

(1) By opening the speech as he does, he immediately wins the attention of the jury to the key point in the defence. He only spoke to

them yesterday; what can he have to say which is new today? He is saying, 'Here am I, one of the most famous advocates of the day, renowned for brains and acumen, and I cannot understand what the prosecution case is.

He then in the course of his statement of facts spells out that Mr Morland alone did what he is alleged to have aided and abetted Lord Kylsant to do; and he did what he did deliberately; and he did what anyone in his profession would have done, had they been in his shoes. That is a complete defence to the charge in fact and in law.

(2)   He makes a very strong emotional appeal to the sense of justice of the jury by putting into plain words what a terrible strain the case must be to Mr Morland. His language is subdued, which enhances the effect.

(3)   In keeping with the whole tone of the speech the peroration is undramatic and depends for its effect on the staggering fact that Mr Morland still does not know what he is supposed to have done wrong.

In its brevity, simplicity, and concentration on the only point in the case this is a classic example of what a defence speech ought to be.

Mr Morland was acquitted.

Appendix 2

IN THE HIGH COURT OF JUSTICE   C0/312
QUEEN'S BENCH DIVISION
CROWN OFFICE LIST

R v SECRETARY OF STATE FOR THE ENVIRONMENT

ex parte BOSTON PORT AUTHORITY

APPLICANT'S SKELETON ARGUMENT

(Page references are to the paginated bundle; tab references are to
the bundle of authorities)

Time estimate: 2 days

INTRODUCTION

1.1   This is an application by the Boston Port Authority ('the Port') for judicial review of a decision of the Secretary of State evidenced in a letter dated 13 July 1994 (page 65) to designate the Indus and Ganges Estuaries as a Special Protection Area ('SPA') and a Ramsar site but not to exclude from the area of the SPA an area within the River Indus upstream of the jurisdictional boundary of the Nile Haven Authority and the Port Authority ('the disputed area').

LEGISLATIVE FRAMEWORK
2.1   By Article 2 of Council Directive 79/409 of 2nd April 1979 ('the Birds Directive' see Tab B) Member States are required 'to take the requisite measures to maintain the population of the species referred to in Article 1 at a level which corresponds in particular to ecological, scientific and cultural requirements while taking account of economic and recreational requirements . . .'

2.2   For the species listed in Annex I to the Birds Directive, Article 4(1) requires Member States to 'classify in particular the most suitable territories in number and size as special protection areas for the conservation of these species . . .'

2.3   Article 4.2 provides that Member States are required to take similar measures for regularly occurring migratory species not listed in Annex I to the Birds Directive and to this end to pay particular attention to the protection of wetlands and particularly to wetlands of international importance.

2.4   Article 6 of Council Directive 92/43/EEC of 21 May 1992 ('the Habitats Directive') provides that a Member State:

(1)   is to establish the necessary conservation measures for an SPA including if appropriate management plans;
(2)   is to take steps to avoid the deterioration of habitats and disturbance of species in SPAs;
(3)   may derogate from that obligation and permit a plan or project provided:

(a)   it has carried out an assessment of the implications for the site;
(b)   there is no alternative solution to carrying out the plan or project;
(c)   there are 'imperative reasons of overriding public interest, including those of a social or economic nature' justifying the plan or project; and
(d)   appropriate nature compensation measures are adopted.

BACKGROUND
3.1   On 27 November 1993, English Nature informed the Port that it was reconsulting on behalf of the Department of Environment on the proposed designation of the Indus and Ganges as an SPA (page 69).

3.2   Following protracted correspondence (see Howell affidavit paras. 14–32, pages 16–20), the Port formally objected to designation by letter dated 17 November 1993 (page 84).

3.3   By letter of 14 June 1994 (see page 57), English nature advised the Respondent that:

(1)   the passage of commercial shipping caused shipwash which was likely to have a significant effect on the SPA but further assessments on the extent of the significance for the estuary as a whole were necessary;
(2)   dredging operations were likely to cause damage to the SPA. In the past that damage had been significant. Its effect in future would depend on how the dredging operations were conducted.

3.4   By letter of 27 June 1994 (page 60), the Respondent informed the Port that it could *not* give an assurance that designation would not affect the Port's operations as shipwash could cause significant damage to bird habitat.

3.5   The Port reiterated its objections to designation because of the effect on the commercial viability of the Port (see letter of 7 July 1994 at page 62).

3.6   The Secretary of State's decision is set out in a letter dated 13 July 1994 at page 65. He decided:

(1)   to designate the area of the Indus and the Ganges as an SPA;
(2)   to exclude 32 hectares required for the expansion of Blacton as the ornithological interest in that 32 hectares was outweighed by economic considerations;
(3)   to exclude 2 other areas; but
(4)   not to exclude the disputed area.

3.7   His reasons for not excluding the disputed area are set out at paragraph 12 of the letter as follows:

'12.   Ministers have now considered representations from Boston Port Authority (IPA) to the effect that the area within the River Ganges upstream of the HHA/IPA jurisdictional boundary should be excluded from the SPA. IPA contend that inclusion of this area within the SPA will inhibit the commercial operation of the Port of Boston in that the passage of shipping and the dredging of the channel may be precluded or restricted to prevent significant harm from taking place to bird habitat. Ministers take the view that there is no clear evidence that these activities would cause significant damage to the ornithological interest for which the site is designated. Ministers expect these issues to be addressed in a management scheme for the area that takes account of the conservation interests, safety factors and IPA's economic interests. Ministers are aware of the derogation procedures available under Article of the Habitats Directive to take account of public safety and economic considerations which area of an overriding public interest.'

THE PROPER APPROACH

4.1   The Birds Directive contemplates two distinct stages. First there is designation under Article 4.1 and 4.2 of the most suitable territories and determination of their precise boundaries. Secondly there is the possibility of derogation from the obligations existing in relation to designated sites (under Article 4(4) of the Birds Directive and its replacement in Article 6 of the Habitats Directive).

4.2   In deciding whether to designate, and in particular in fixing the boundaries of an SPA, the Secretary of State is required to weigh the ornithological interest of the disputed area with the economic interests of the Port. The Court of Appeal (A and B LJJ; C LJ dissenting) has held that the Respondent is required to perform a balancing exercise weighing the ornithological interest against the economic interest. *R* v *Secretary of State for the Environment ex p. RSPB* Tab J at page 26F–27E; 47A–B. The House of Lords has referred to the European Court the question of whether the Respondent is entitled to have regard to economic considerations in designating an SPA and defining its boundaries: Tab K.

4.3   In the present case, the Secretary of State did carry out that exercise in relation to the area at Felixstowe where, in paragraphs 4 to 11 the economic case for excluding an area of 32 acres required by Blacton and weighed that interest against the specific ornithological interest in that 32 acres (see pages 66–67).

4.4   In the case of the Port, the Secretary of State erred in law in that he did not carry out such a balancing exercise as appears from each of the following, namely:

(1)   given the material before him, there was no basis upon which the Respondent could reasonably conclude that there was no clear evidence that designation would not have an effect upon the commercial operation of the Port and consequently failed to weigh that interest in deciding whether to designate;

(2)   given the material and the evidence of the risk of significant damage to the operation of the Port, the proper approach for the Respondent was to have weighed the risk of significant damage against the ornithological interest; and

(3)   the Respondent proceeded on the basis, erroneous in law, that if there were an effect upon the economic interests of the Port that could be accommodated within a management plan or a derogation from the obligations which attach to designation, rather than engaging in a balancing exercise weighing the ornithological interest and the economic interest;

(4)   the Respondent failed to consider the ornithological interest in the disputed area in deciding whether to include or exclude that area within the boundaries of the SPA.

NO EVIDENCE

5.1   There was no basis, given the material before him, upon which the Secretary of State could conclude that there was no clear evidence that the passage of shipping and dredging would cause significant harm to the Port or alternatively the Secretary of State could not reasonably come to that conclusion on the evidence before him as appears from the following:

(1)   the advice upon which ministers proceeded was that contained in the English Nature letter of 14 June 1994 (see Smith aff. para. 6 page 32);

(2)   that advice was clearly to the effect that (a) shipwash would have a significant effect upon the SPA and (b) dredging would cause damge which had in the past been significant and whether it would do so in future depended on how the dredging was carried out;

(3)   the Respondent refused to give an assurance on 27 June 1994 that designation would not affect the Port precisely because of the likely significant damage from shipwash;

(4)   those conclusions were confirmed by the Port's own representations of 7 July 1994 (see page 62);

(5)   the Respondent accepts (Smith aff. paras 10 and pages 34–35) that the advice was that shipwash was likely to have a significant effect and that the possibility that the economic activity of the Port would be affected could not be excluded;

(6)   in the circumstances, the suggestion that the significance of shipwash was unclear (Smith para. 10 pages 34–35) or could not be quantified (para. 11 pages 35–36) or that the significance remained to be assessed (para. 12 page 37) is misleading and incorrect. In the light of the evidence, it was clear that shipwash was causing significant damage to the mudflats. The precise extent of that effect (that is *how* significant it was) remained to be assessed. No evidence has been produced to suggest that shipwash did not cause damage or that the damage was not significant;

(7)   so far as dredging is concerned, the advice was that it was likely to cause damage. That had been significant in the past; whether it would be in future depended on the nature of the operation. The significance depended upon a number of factors to be assessed. Given that advice, the minister could only reasonably proceed on the basis that there was likely to be a significant effect, or at best, that further enquiries as to the likely risk of significant damage had to be made. It does not support the conclusion that there was no clear evidence of significant damage. Further, the reference to assessment in English Nature's was made and understood by the Respondent to be made in the context of considering giving consent in future to a derogation from the obligation attaching to a designated area (see Respondent's letter of 27 June 1994 page 60). It is not advice that dredging may not need to be carried out in a way that causes significant damage to the SPA. It is not in any way advice that the risk of significant damage can be assessed in future and avoided by appropriate methods so that designation need have no effect on the Port;

(8)   in the premises, there was no basis for the conclusion that there was no clear evidence that shipping would cause significant harm as set out in the decision letter and paragraph 12 of Donald affidavit (page 37).

5.2   As a result of this, the Respondent erred in concluding that there was no clear evidence that designation would harm the commercial operation of the Port. As a consequence, he failed to assess the damage to the commercial operation of the Port that designation would have, in particular its effect on shipwash and dredging. Given the nature of the evidence before him, the proper approach for the Secretary of State was to assess the risk of significant damage to the commercial operation of the Port and to weigh that together with the ornithological interest of the disputed area in deciding whether to designate and, if so, whether to include or exclude the disputed area. In the premises, he did not weigh the damage to economic interests within the meaning of Article 2 at the stage of deciding whether to designate or what the boundaries of the SPA should be.

MISCONSTRUCTION OF ARTICLE 6

6.1   The Respondent proceeded on the basis that if there were any damage to the economic interests of the Port, that could be dealt with by:

(a)   a management plan or
(b)   derogation, both provided for by Article 6 of the Habitats Directive.

See decision letter and Donald affidavit para. 11 page 36.

Management Plans

6.2   The Respondent erred in considering that economic interests could be considered under a management plan. Such plans are an aspect of the necessary conservation measures adopted under Article 6(1) of the Habitats Directive. They are intended to correspond to the ecological requirements of the habitats and species on the site. They are not a vehicle for assessing economic interests. That is to be assessed at the designation stage, or if a site has already been designated, by way of a derogation under Articles 6(3) and (4) of the Habitats Directive.

6.3   In so far as the minister is referring to a non-statutory plan (see para. 8 of Smith page 34), such a plan could not be used as a means of qualifying the obligations in the Birds Directive. The economic interests are either taken into account at the designation stage or at the derogation stage. There is no intermediate 'non-statutory' mechanism by which Community law obligations are qualified by reference to economic considerations.

Derogation
6.4   The possibility of taking account of the economic interests of the
Port by way of a derogation is not a justification for failure to perform
the balancing exercise at the designation stage as:

(1)   the purpose of designation is to assess which sites are the most
suitable, bearing in mind considerations both of the conservation interest
and the economic interest recognised by Article 2 of the Birds Directive;
(2)   derogation is possible only if there is no alternative, an
assessment has been conducted, the reasons for departing from an
already recognised SPA are imperative and overriding, and appropriate compensation measures are adopted; it is no substitute for the
proper exercise of discretion at the designation stage;
(3)   further, derogation will only deal with matters such as dredging
on an ad hoc basis; the designation stage is meant to be the stage at
which a global view of the relative merits of the ornithological and
economic interest is taken. If the matter is left to derogation, there will
be continuing uncertainty as to whether a particular operation would
be allowed in future. The designation exercise (if favourable) would
determine that question for the Port.

Conclusion
6.5   By reason of the decision to assess the economic interest by way of
a management plan or derogation, the Respondent failed to carry out the
balancing exercise required at the designation stage, namely identifying
the economic interest of the Port and the ornithological interest and
balancing the two in deciding whether to designate and if so, what the
boundaries should be.

6.6   Further, in so far as the Respondent suggests that there is no duty
to consider economic interests merely a discretion to do so, should the
Secretary of State so wish (Smith para. 13 page 37) that is no answer to
the present application as:

(1)   the Respondent has never sought to suggest that the present case
is not one where it is inappropriate to consider economic interests;
(2)   the Respondent has sought to take account of those interests in
part in relation to Blacton;
(3)   Article 2 of the Birds Directive does require (not merely permits)
the Respondent to have regard to economic interests.

THE ORNITHOLOGICAL INTEREST
7.1   In deciding whether to designate, and a fortiori, in fixing the precise boundaries and deciding whether to include or exclude the disputed area, the Respondent is required to consider the ornithological interest in that disputed area (not the proposed SPA as a whole) to determine whether the economic interests of the Port outweigh the ornithological interests in that area.

7.2   The Respondent undertook that exercise relation to the exclusion of the 32 hectares at Hotton Hills (see para 5 of the decision letter of 13 July 1994 at page 66 and the Respondents's letter of 25 May 1994 to English Nature) and the areas of open water in the Ganges and on the side of Hand Quay (see paras 9 and 11 of the decision letter).

7.3   The decision letter does not assess the ornithological interest of the disputed area but simply refers to the ornithological interest of site as a whole. Further, the Respondent does not state in his affidavit that the ornithological interest of the disputed area was considered and weighed together with the economic interest of the Port. Rather, it states that in ecological terms the Ganges and the Indus could be regarded together and that bird counts were available for the Ganges see Smith aff. para 8. page 34 (the Respondent has refused to indicate whether these bird counts were before the Minister: see correspondence at DAH 2 pages 285 to 292). In any event, there is no suggestion that there was any attempt to identify the ornithological interest of the disputed area in deciding whether or not to include it within or exclude it from the SPA.

CONCLUSIONS
8.1   At present, the House of Lords has referred to the European Court the question of whether the Birds Directive permits the Respondent to have regard to economic considerations in classifying an area as an SPA and in defining its boundaries: *R* v *Secretary of State for the Environment ex p. RSPB* Tab K page 6.

8.2   The Port's case is that the Secretary of State was required or at least entitled to take account of the Port's economic interests in deciding whether to designate and, if so, what the precise boundaries of the SPA should be. He failed properly to do so for the following separate reasons:

(1)   there was no material before him upon which he could reasonably conclude that there was no clear evidence that designation would have an affect on the commercial operations of the Port; given the material before him, the proper approach was to conclude that there was evidence of such damage or that there was a risk of significant damage;
(2)   rather than engaging in a balancing exercise weighing the economic and the environmental basis, he proceeded on the basis, erroneous in law, that the interests could be accommodated in a management plan or could be taken account of at the derogation stage rather than the designation stage;
(3)   he failed to assess the ornithological interest in the disputed area in deciding whether to include or exclude the disputed area from the SPA.

8.3   If any of these arguments succeeds, then the decision of the Respondent is flawed on the basis that the current state of the law is that economic interests are to be taken into account. Consequently, the decision should be quashed and the matter remitted to the Respondent.

8.4   Alternatively, if it is considered that the decision should not be quashed until it is known whether the European Court rules that economic considerations can be taken into account at the designation stage, the court should refer the following questions, in addition to those referred by the House of Lords:

(1)   may a Member State take account of the economic consider-ations mentioned in Article 2 of Council Directive 79/409/EEC when establishing the necessary conservation measures including a manage-ment plan within the meaning of Article 6(1) of Council Directive 92/43/EEC?
(2)   is a Member State required or merely entitled to take account of the considerations mentioned in Article 2 of Council Directive 79/409/EEC in classification an area as a Special Protection Area and/or in defining the boundaries of such an area pursuant to Article 4(1) and/or 4(2) of the Directive?

A. JONES QC
C. WILLIAMS

Notes.

(1)   It is important to bear in mind that the main purpose of skeleton arguments is to assist the judge to understand the main contentions in the case, in law and in fact; and to clarify the essential issues.

(2)   That it is not helpful to expound the whole of your case in the skeleton. It should be the bare bones. The quickened flesh and blood remains for oral presentation.

(3)   It is an effective use of the opportunity you have of stating your case, to highlight your best points and if you have a knock down argument to unleash it.

(4)   Great care should always be taken in summarising a document or authority to do it accurately and concisely. If you do it ineptly your credibility with the judge is likey to be undermined.

(5)   Your skeleton should not be read out. It should be used for reference. In the usual case there will be a skeleton on the other side. You will be able to see what the real issues are when the opposing arguments are laid side by side. You can then use your skeleton to refer to matters which are common ground, or which need no elaboration. The object really is to cut down the oral submissions to the core of the dispute by providing the judge with all the information which will enable him to grapple with the central issues.